My Red Couch

and Other Stories on Seeking a Feminist Faith

My Red Couch

and Other Stories on Seeking a Feminist Faith

CLAIRE BISCHOFF
AND RACHEL GAFFRON
Editors

The Pilgrim Press
Cleveland

Dedication

To all those who have come before us in this tensegritous conversation: we are indebted to your contributions.

To all those who continue to seek an authentic path of Christian faith and social justice defined by contemporary feminism: may you know that there are many voices to challenge, support, and encourage you on the journey.

To all future sojourners searching for a feminist faith: may our conversation inspire and influence your own.

The Pilgrim Press, 700 Prospect Avenue, Cleveland, Ohio 44115-1100
thepilgrimpress.com

Printed in the United States of America on acid-free paper

09   08   07   06   05   5   4   3   2   1

Library of Congress Cataloging-in-Publication Data

My red couch-and other stories on seeking a feminist faith /
    Claire E. Bischoff and Rachel Gaffron, editors.
        p. cm.
    Includes bibliographical references.
    ISBN 0-8298-1670-4 (alk. paper)
    1. Feminists—Religious life.   2. Young women—Religious life.
3. Feminism—Religious aspects—Christianity.   I. Bischoff, Claire E., 1978–
II. Gaffron, Rachel, 1975–
BV4596.F4M9 2005
270.8'3'082—dc22

                                                                2005022506

Contents

Acknowledgments

We extend heartfelt thanks to:

The Re-Imagining Conference planners and participants, who provided the forum for our initial conversation on the ambiguities of faith and feminism.

Dr. Mary Bednarowski, who introduced us to each other and provided constructive feedback on an early draft of the manuscript. We appreciate your willingness to listen to our generation's struggles to reconcile feminism and faith.

Pamela Johnson, who heard our stories and recognized the importance of this conversation in the larger community. You entrusted us with your seedling idea to bring together the voices of young Christian feminists, and we are honored by your belief in us.

Dr. Rita Nakashima Brock, who graciously wrote the foreword, framing our project with a passion for social change to which we also aspire.

Jenny Kipka, who donated her time to a careful proofreading of our manuscript in its final stages.

Ulrike Guthrie at The Pilgrim Press for embracing our project with enthusiasm.

Claire specifically expresses gratitude for:

My husband, Ethan—you supported this project even though you knew that my hours in front of the computer would mean fewer hours with you, and you believed in me even when I had trouble believing in myself.

My parents, Margaret and Michael, and my siblings, Ellie, Maggie, Patrick, and Murphy—you provide the loving foundation of my life, allow me to be myself, and remind me of the importance of fun and laugher.

The PSITs and the Raider girls—you grant me much needed breaks from my rather solitary academic world, reminding me what a true blessing friendship is.

My mentors and faculty advisors—Dr. Edmund Santurri, Dr. Mary Hess, Dr. Mary Elizabeth Moore, and Joy Biedrzycki—and the faculties at Cretin-Derham Hall High School, St. Olaf College, Luther Seminary, and Emory University—you have challenged me theologically and inspired me with your lived commitment to faith and your dynamic way of sharing your faith with your students.

Rachel specifically expresses gratitude for:

My husband, William—your unconditional love and belief in me make the writing life possible and regular life joy-filled.

All of my family—your generosity and spirit shape my life. My parents, Barbara and David, and my sister, Elizabeth—you honor my aspirations, and I cherish our conversations and laughter.

The supportive writing community in the Twin Cities, including my dear ally Anne; Angela, Anita, and Mary of the Tuesday Group; the encouraging vibe and people of the Loft Literary Center; and Trudy, who listened to early drafts of what I needed to say.

The kindness of many, including RED group for sustained creative encouragement and spiritual friendship; Genie and Susan for cheering me on; and the generous philanthropy of Joan Drury and the Norcroft Writing Retreat for Women.

We offer our deep thanks to all of the family, friends, and colleagues who helped to advertise our book in its infancy. It is because of your hard work that the response to this project was even greater than anticipated.

Thank you to each and every person who wrote an essay to be considered for this volume. Your voices helped to shape and challenge the manuscript, and we hope you are inspired to continue the conversation.

Foreword

❁

*T*hroughout U.S. history, from the abolitionists and suffragists of the nineteenth century to the feminists and civil rights activists of the twentieth, progressive religious people have served as advocates of humane and democratic values. A renewed progressive interfaith movement coalesced in the fall of 2004 around the election. The current movement is sorely in need of the courageous young women whose stories fill this book. They are crucial to the success of progressive Christianity and the larger faith legacy to which it belongs.

These young women came of age during an orchestrated backlash against progressive religion. Over two decades ago, secular hardright foundations, such as Coors, Olin, Bradley, and Scaife, founded five nonprofit think tanks to move religion rightward. These well-funded think tanks seek to convey a sense of a nationwide moral decay, based on a morality narrowly defined around family and sex. They attempt to undergird capitalism with the ethics of market fundamentalism. They support policies that use religious organizations to distribute government assistance funds and that undermine public support for the common good. They seek to affect public policy toward conservative ends, and their right-wing advocacy groups within mainline churches have moved them rightward.[1] The women in this book experienced the double whammy of the religious right's attempt to hijack Christianity and the secular academy, which is often disdainful of religion as a bad gene or viral infection.

The Institute for Religion and Democracy (IRD) targeted the feminist movement called "Re-Imagining," a community of feminist Christians that was born after the 1993 World Council of Churches' mid-decade celebration of Churches in Solidarity with Women, attended by 2000 women. This book emerged from Re-Imagining, and the women brought together by this collection are one of the movement's most important legacies.

I write this following a summit of progressive religious leaders organized in December 2004. I am convinced a renewed progressive Christianity must include the strength, spiritual insight, and leadership of the women who speak here. These intelligent, thoughtful, willful women embody the religious values and activism that have been the bedrock of civil society. They bring a complex, nuanced, and less polemicized feminism to the struggle. They are not paralyzed by contradictions, ambiguities, and struggle, but find spiritual strength in complexity. Their feminist commitments have greater equilibrium for staying power over the long haul, captured in their use of the word *tensegrity*, the strength that comes from holding contrary notions.

From church pews to library carrels, from the tear gas of political demonstrations to the wails of an infant, and from writer's pen to elevated pulpit, these women speak to a new generation of feminist Christians. They invite a conversation with sister-travelers seeking to be faithful to themselves, to each other, to their communities, to their religious inheritance, to their feminist commitments, and to their best, most creative work. I am grateful they invited me to read their stories, to overhear their honest struggle for wholeness in a deeply broken world—a world that is far better for their being in it. They offer me more than hope. They give me confidence in the future of both feminism and Christianity.

—*Rita Nakashima Brock*

Introduction—In Search of a Feminist Faith

*D*o you feel alone in your search to be a feminist and a Christian? Does it often feel impossible to reconcile these two seemingly disparate ideologies? Do you ever have feelings of doubt or disillusionment about your faith tradition? And what does it mean to be a feminist anyway?

My Red Couch—and Other Stories on Seeking a Feminist Faith is a catalyst to aid you in the journey toward answering these questions, as well as to encourage you to be creative in your response. Within this book are the personal stories of twenty-four young people who are grappling with the complex claim of a Christian feminist identity. These are the stories of women who are single, married, gay, and straight. These are the stories of mothers and daughters, students and young professionals. These are the stories of devout women, as well as those who can no longer worship regularly with their church family. There is even a story by a woman and her boyfriend, a man who is as devoted as she is to a contemporary feminist movement because he, too, believes passionately in the equal rights of all God's people.

It is our hope that *My Red Couch—and Other Stories on Seeking a Feminist Faith* will inspire you to create forums in which to reconcile feminism with faith traditions. It takes great intention to acknowledge the challenges of the modern world, and our generation must begin a dialogue about the complexity of constructing personal identity in order to create visionary communities that are the foundation of positive social change. The architect Buckminster Fuller used the word *tensegrity* to describe the paradoxical integrity of opposing forces—that is, the strength lent to a structure by competing tensions. It is our experience that feminism and Christian faith are often interpreted as negatively opposed when, in truth, their paradoxical relationship provides invaluable strength to us personally and communally.

This unique volume of narrative essays was written by young Christian feminists between the ages of twenty-one and thirty-five. It is divided into four parts, each of which focuses on one of the following "in search of" themes: integrity, community, creativity, and tensegrity. We selected these categories to highlight different elements of the spiritual journey toward integrating feminism and faith. The integrity section includes essays dealing specifically with stories of constructing personal identity. Here a deeply spiritual woman shares her struggle of working in an English department that considers Christianity obsolete. Another young woman narrates her story of healing from anorexia by embracing her whole self: feminist and Christian. Similarly, two other authors discuss how the self can feel compromised when embracing both Christian and feminist identities. This section concludes with the story of a newly ordained clergywoman who wrestles honestly with the novelty of motherhood.

Essays in the community section discuss the joys and challenges of finding spiritual communities that uphold feminist ideals. One author calls herself "a walking contradiction" as an African American woman who longs for the cultural home of a black church while remaining uncomfortable with its conservative understanding of gender roles. Two different Catholic voices discuss the complexity of staying in a denomination that denies women full participation, while a young Episcopal priest tells of her hesitancy to be openly Christian with strangers. One woman observes the spiritual quality of water that connects humanity, and another author reminisces on the ironies of the evangelical community in which she was raised. Both the integrity and community sections are followed by questions and visioning exercises to encourage you to write the narrative of your own search for a feminist faith and to find a community that supports it.

When we create space in our lives for feminism and faith to coexist, we become individuals of integrity and communities of strength. Creativity's presence is necessary for such a tensegritous relationship to work. Like the other sections in this book, the creativity section includes essays by authors from a variety of backgrounds. One woman shares her imaginative mélange of spiritual disciplines, including the astrology of her Mayan ancestors and the veneration of the Virgin Mary. A poet playfully asks readers to consider looking for the extraordinary in the ordinary and discovers a connection to the Divine in her own creative process. In another essay, a girlfriend and boyfriend dialogue about the influence of Christianity and feminism on their understanding of gender roles. The importance of seeing and interpreting Christian metaphors in new ways, as well as experimenting with visual media as a spiritual discipline, is at the heart of several essays in this section.

All of the essays in this book could in some way fit into the tensegrity section, but we chose the six essays here based on the tensegrity between the author's feminism and faith in relationship to greater cultural issues. In the book's final essay, its author shares her experience at the 2004 March for Women's Lives, during which she witnessed the hateful misunderstanding directed toward those attending as prochoice Christians. Another author finds her feminism challenged while experiencing "a dark night of the soul," for which she finds no solace in her feminist theology, but rather in a text that acknowledges the possibility of growth through pain. Here, too, is an essay by a woman most spiritually at home in the Church of Jesus Christ of Latter-Day Saints in which she was raised, as well as one by an Episcopal clergywoman struggling with prejudice toward female leadership.

Following the tensegrity as well as the creativity sections are topical discussion questions and action activities to encourage you to integrate the visioning exercises from the previous sections into your personal journey toward a feminist faith. The words and the ideas in this book are an invitation to you to join in this timely conversation, to gather and to discuss what it means to be a Christian, what it means to be a feminist, and how to reconcile the two.

THE GENESIS OF THIS BOOK

We owe our friendship to Dr. Mary Bednarowski, professor emerita of Religious Studies at United Theological Seminary of the Twin Cities in New Brighton, Minnesota. Mary was a long-time friend of the Re-Imagining community, which began in 1993 after a conference sponsored by the Minnesota Council of Churches in response to the World Council of Churches' Decade in Solidarity with Women. The overwhelming response to the conference inspired the creation of a nonprofit organization that encouraged lay and clergy to "re-imagine" more inclusive and contemporary ways of relating to God, creating community, and interpreting ritual. Rachel, as one of the conference organizers, invited Mary to speak at the tenth anniversary Re-Imagining event held in spring of 2003. Conversation was a major theme of this anniversary celebration, and the planning committee hoped Mary would ask two of her students to present an intergenerational discussion about feminism and Christianity. Claire was the first student who came to mind.

Earlier that year, Claire had registered for a course Mary was offering entitled, "The History of Women in American Religion." When the original course had to be canceled due to a lack of interest, Mary graciously agreed to lead an independent study despite Claire's enrollment at a different institution. Throughout that semester, Claire and Mary started a conversation on the ironies and ambivalences of women's religious experiences, as Claire recurrently encountered similar refrains in the writing of women from different eras, ethnicities, and denominations. While Claire and Mary conversed about weekly assignments via e-mail, Mary was also meeting with Rachel and the other conference planners in the year leading up to the Re-Imagining anniversary celebration. During the planning team's monthly meetings, Rachel shared her feelings of frustration about her generation's lack of community and disinterest in feminism. Mary heard another voice that needed to participate in the dialogue that she and Claire had begun.

Both of us were deeply honored by Mary's invitation to share the podium with her. The three of us met frequently to discuss our stories as religious women and to discern themes that might be common among our experiences. Together we wondered about the contemporary results of the social changes of the last forty years: Why aren't there more students interested in taking a course on women and religion? Why are there so few young women involved in a contemporary feminist movement? Is feminism necessary anymore? What is the relationship between feminist beliefs and our Christian heritage? Why aren't there more conversations between mothers and daughters about the enormous changes that have occurred in the last four decades? And why—despite a thirty-year age difference—were our stories of experiential sexism so hauntingly similar to Mary's? Today equal rights are a normal part of our social dialogue, yet children are still subjected to—though often through elusively subtle messages—this paralyzing theme: girls are not as human as boys. Daily we are assaulted with images of women objectified, hypersexualized, and culturally undervalued. How does the church participate in these lessons?

On the day of the conference, the weather itself felt like a blessing. The sun shone deep and clear in an azure sky. For us it was a day of initiation. We both took the stage sweaty with nerves. We had little experience speaking to crowds of two hundred people, but there was no turning back. We needed the calm and belief of our mentor, Mary, to lead us in speaking our personal truths. It was a powerful experience to state our ambiguous relationship with religion, as well as with feminism. We spoke about Christianity and feminism in honor of our mothers' generation, as well as to voice our struggles to our peers. The audience responded to our stories with laughter and tears. Our words gave voice to the emotions of many of those gathered. We were mutually grateful for a passionate standing ovation at the close of our session.

During the question and answer period, a recent high school graduate approached the microphone. She was one of the youngest women in the room and thanked us for sharing our stories. Not until that day had she known it was possible to speak of her feminism and her faith in the same sentence. But she also asked: "Where are the other young women?" We celebrated the opportunity to connect with the young women in the audience, but we also mourned the small number of young attendees. Unbeknown to us, another wise mentor was in the audience that day. Pamela Johnson, an editor at The Pilgrim Press, recognized that our stories had the power to touch the lives of more young women. She heard the young graduate's question and approached us with one of her own: "What if you two create a collection of young Christian women's stories about faith and feminism?"

We spent the next two months putting together a project proposal that would bring to life Pamela's vision. In doing so, we researched other titles on the market, only to discover how few existed on the topic of young women and Christian feminism. Together, we shared a longing for a Christian church that would take seriously the wellspring of the contemporary feminist movement as an influence for transformation. Gender equality, we noted, is a far larger issue than the ordination of women. We shared our dream of a book that would encourage conversation about how faith and feminism are understood in this country. We recognized that a creative synthesis between feminism and faith, however paradoxical, would inspire positive change for future generations. Thus our path in search of a feminist faith began. We are calling the Christian church to live up to its proclamation that women and men are created equal in the image of God. We are calling our society to live up to its promises of liberty and justice for all.

Ironically, Christianity and feminism as social institutions share many qualities. Both groups are sabotaged by the consumer media culture. Both groups have been pronounced "dead" by postmodernism. Both groups share a radical message of equality and justice that falls upon the deaf ears of capitalism. Both groups have difficulty organizing and sustaining themselves to respond creatively to the fatigue of social justice organizations and the apathy of many young Americans. Both groups have factions that denounce the importance of the other's purpose, as evidenced by actions like several mainstream denominations' decisions to cut funding for their Committee on the Status of Women or the neighborhood feminist group that ignores the spiritual heritage of Christianity in reaction to the patriarchy of its institution. In this volume you will meet people who refuse to settle for an easy compromise between their feminist and Christian beliefs. Here the misperception that "feminism" is a bad word is challenged. Here the misconstruction that to be religious in the United States today is to be a fervent fundamentalist is denied. In our "either/or" culture, we hope the stories in this collection offer ways to be "both/and"—both a feminist and a Christian.

YOUNG, FEMINIST, AND CHRISTIAN: WHY THESE PARAMETERS?

The voices of young women are included in this volume to bring a focus to our particular generational experience. Despite our generation's reputation for cultural apathy, we recognize that many twenty-somethings experience a "quarter-life crisis" in which they seek opportunities to ask some of life's bigger questions. While our parents' generations found community support in traditional church circles or political movements, we ourselves often lack physical communities in which to address our concerns about current culture.

We are a transient generation that moves often and rarely establishes roots in our new environs. We are saturated in a media cynicism that undermines our cultural institutions. We are overwhelmed by global concerns that include the enormity of environmental degradation and the degeneration in the quality of life for the world's citizens. We live in an ever-changing world of pluralism in which there is a constant blending of trends and traditions. Yet as human beings it is natural to long for a connection to the rituals that ground us in a historical community. As the false message of "you can have it all" echoes from our television screens, many young people are in want of a more reasonable way to compose a life.

We cherish the generations who have come before us for their groundbreaking work of connecting the feminist movement with Christian inheritance. We encourage cross-generational conversations, respecting that many stories from the women's movement in the late 1960s and the 1970s have gone unheard. We ask for mutual respect to be practiced between the generations. If anything, this book is proof that feminist conversation and issues are alive and well. This is often a disappointing—sometimes surprising—conclusion to women who sacrificed much during what is often called the "second wave" of the contemporary feminist movement during the civil rights period. Our generation blissfully profits from changed laws and attitudes towards women's roles. But we do have a significant way to go before "equal rights" are attained in our culture. Our generation has a particular set of challenges to overcome, including its own ignorance about the past.

Some feminists of our generation seek to define themselves as a specific community by claiming the title of "third wave," an assertion as the third major movement of feminism in the United States. The "first wave" began in 1848 with the Declaration of Rights and Sentiments at Seneca Falls that spurred the seventy-two year struggle for women's right to vote. African American women were not guaranteed suffrage under the law until the civil rights movement during what is considered the "second wave" of contemporary feminism. Though suffrage was the major focus of "first wave" American feminism, one could count up to nine generations of women working toward voting rights until the Nineteenth Amendment was passed in 1920—and up to thirteen generations of women working toward voting rights for all.

Many women in our own generation do not identify with the title of "third wave" feminism, yet issues like equal pay for equal work still echo from our mothers' "second wave" demonstrations to our own. Unlike many of our mothers' groups, "third wave" feminists are often more willing to include men in the feminist conversation, as well as to tackle issues of gender and sexuality. Critics of "third-wave" feminism discount it for its focus on individualism and with relief recognize a new wave of feminism on the horizon. This "fourth wave" designates itself with a joyful, globally inspired feminism that draws wisdom from women's spirituality. In the April 2005 issue of *Utne Reader*, Pythia Peay explains in her article "Feminism's Fourth Wave" that women across faiths are gathering together to "explore a new feminine paradigm of power that's based on tolerance, mutuality, and reverence for nature—values they now see as crucial to curing the global pathologies of poverty and war." We applaud the optimism and enthusiasm of women—and men—participating in a global activism infused with spirituality.

It is our hope that *My Red Couch* will help facilitate such work. As one young woman at the Re-Imagining conference put it: no matter which wave, we are all one body of water. Nevertheless, this is a collection of young voices, almost all women. We recognized a need for a more contemporary collection of Christian feminist stories, yet are challenged by the complexity of male participation in feminist discussion. We do not often encounter women in our age bracket who are willing to call themselves feminists, let alone men. All of us need to encourage one another to nurture the ability to articulate one's inherent power and inherited role within society. Finding our voice is the first crucial step toward change, and often we women only find the courage to seek empowerment within the company of other women.

Our feminism is based on a core belief that women and men were created in the image of God. Any aspect of society that denies this truth needs to be challenged. We also recognize that in many circles, feminism functions as a second "f" word. In common parlance, feminists are those who hate men and who cause trouble. We believe that this volume will challenge cultural images of what it means to be a feminist. When we refer to feminism, we draw on bell hooks's definition of feminism as the movement to eliminate sexism through the acquisition of equal rights, opportunities, and treatment.[1] Feminism is a holistic category that influences all areas of our lives, including religion. As long as women are paid less on the dollar than men for doing the same job, as long as women are saddled with the majority of childrearing and cleaning work, as long as women are demeaned in the media as sexual objects, there is still a place for feminism in our society. Our cultural understanding of gender roles needs to evolve in order for intrinsic social change to occur. As long as women are considered a husband's property within the covenant of marriage, as long as women are denied positions of public religious leadership, as long as the patriarchy of the Christian church denies or mystifies the spiritual quality of women, as long as Christianity ignores feminine metaphors for God, there is still a place for feminism in our households of faith.

When we refer to "faith," we mean reliance on or trust in a transcendent being or power, generally experienced as a belief in something greater than ourselves.[2] We recognize that faith takes different forms in people's lives and that it need not be connected to institutional religion. Faith is about where our heart is, what gives our life meaning, and what impels us to action. One of the most difficult decisions we had to make in conceiving this book was whether or not it should be a collection of interfaith stories. We advocate the importance of understanding and promoting religious pluralism, but we also believe it is necessary to understand one's origins in order to be fully articulate in the wider conversation. Claiming a name or a group to define who you are is an entry point into your belief system.

Ultimately, for these reasons, we decided to limit this work to Christianity. We both grew up in the Christian church (Claire is Roman Catholic, and Rachel is a pastor's kid, daughter of a United Methodist minister). We are both comfortable with discussing Christian theology and traditions and felt we were unqualified to edit a work that included essays representing other religions. We recognize the diversity of Christianity within contemporary America and are pleased that these authors were honest in articulating their personal theologies, each as unique as the shapely lines of a person's fingerprint. It is our belief that at its essence Christianity is a religion founded on the principles of a loving God and a radical prophet's wisdom to "love your neighbor as yourself." We do not understand how fundamentalist religious groups— many of them supposedly Christian—can interpret this tenant into a "god-endorsed" hatred toward our gay, lesbian, bisexual, and transgender sisters and brothers; toward minority groups, especially those living in dire poverty; and toward the innocents of nations torn by war, imperialism, and ecological ignorance.

We look forward to reading other essay collections assembled on the complexity of feminism and faith for those practicing other religions, especially young Jewish and Muslim women, whose traditions stem from the same genealogical roots as Christianity. Although we have approached this volume from an explicitly

Christian perspective, we anticipate that our understanding of faith is broad enough to include those of other faith backgrounds in our conversation, as well as those persons who may never before have considered themselves faithful or "religious."

OUR VISION FOR THIS COLLECTION OF STORIES

This book is for anyone who identifies with or has roots in a Christian tradition, who is cognizant of cultural misogyny, and who struggles with the complexity of weaving together an authentic life. This book is for the recent high school graduate who asked, "What is feminism?" at the Re-Imagining conference. It is for the thirty-something who no longer attends traditional worship but is a community activist longing for a spiritual circle. It is for the classroom full of college students studying feminist theology but in need of a more contemporary text that reflects lived experience. It is for the trio of neighborhood friends who gathers at the corner cafe for their monthly book club. And it is for readers of any age who are interested in knowing more about the faith experiences of young women born after the first twenty years or so of "second wave" feminism but whose lives have been affected by it in so many different ways.

These essays were gathered democratically from a national pool of writers, in hopes of acquiring a wide variety of experiences and backgrounds. We advertised with professional writing and religious journals and personally contacted over three hundred seminaries and women's and religious studies programs in North America. We were committed to our promise of a blind jury during the selection process. We thank each and every one of you who wrote for this volume. Your words helped to shape a project idea into what we feel is a cohesive manuscript. We do not claim this book to be the definitive collection on young Christian feminism. What we do know is that the stories you hold in your hand are evidence of the deep need for conversation regarding the topic of faith and feminism.

We have done our best to select essays that represent voices from every region of the United States and are pleased to be including a Korean-Canadian voice, as well. Almost a dozen different denominations are represented in these essays, including Assemblies of God, American Baptist, Church of Jesus Christ of Latter-Day Saints, Episcopal, Lutheran, Presbyterian, Roman Catholic, and United Methodist. There are also authors from nondenominational backgrounds, as well as those who have chosen to no longer associate with a traditional faith community. We hope you will feel a sense of camaraderie while reading the narrative sections of this book.

Story telling is both an empowering and educational activity. By sharing our stories, we validate our experiences, give witness to our personal truths, and open up an intergenerational dialogue. We want you to engage in this dialogue and hope the discussion questions give you an immediate sense of participation. The vision and activity portions of the book are intended to empower you to recognize and develop these important skills. Our dreams in action are what make a difference in this world. We hope our book inspires you to contribute your voice to the larger discussion of how to create a feminist movement that supports spiritual growth and faith communities that honor our personal integrity as women.

We wish you blessings for your journey.

"So what do you do?"

*It's the inevitable question at every company function
Claire attends with her husband. And it's difficult for her
to admit to a group of computer consultants that most of
her time is spent devoted to religious causes. The more she
is suspected of being a fundamentalist fanatic, the more
she wishes to respond with an answer they'll understand.*

"I'm an accountant," she imagines herself saying.

*Similarly, Rachel's determination to claim the elusive title
of artist is greeted with rounds of stereotyped commentary
about insanity, drugs, and unreliability. She answers to
none of these assumptions, but like Claire, still struggles to
sustain the energy it takes to ignore the culture's remarks
on her chosen vocation.*

*How do we as individuals find compatibility in our beliefs
and our actions?*

One

CONFLICT 101

April Heaney

ot long ago, a colleague in the English department remarked off-handedly to me that the "god squad" in her college composition class was at it again— submitting essays that attempted to preach Christian beliefs. "No matter how many times I tell them to consider their audience, they just don't get it. Scripture is not proof to the thinking world." The idea of sharing my own struggles to reconcile scripture with contemporary culture did not cross my mind. I, too, had grimaced over papers that arrogantly asserted fundamentalist doctrine; I had empathized with essays that rejoiced in awkward prose over a conversion experience—envying, to some degree, these students' unabashed proclamation of faith. I gave my colleague a practiced nod and smile.

Because I am a lecturer at a secular university, a feminist, and a devoted Christian, I am no stranger to the complexities of audience consideration. When I entered graduate school in 1998, I began piecing together what felt like a horrid poly-personality of competing loyalties. I was a member of a department comprised of mostly women, all strong feminists whom I admired and wanted to emulate, and none, that I knew of, who were Christian. I had Christian friends and roommates who viewed feminists as a Nazi regime of women who railed against God's ordained gender roles. In the company of both groups, I kept my thoughts to myself, unable to fully articulate my position on either camp—even to myself.

When I read Carolyn Heilbrun's book *Writing a Woman's Life* as part of a course titled "Women in Writing," I drove home after our class discussion feeling as if the bottom had dropped out from under me. Feminism, I thought, cannot truly be in harmony with Christian belief. The passages I had underlined in the book, passages that caught my eye because they pricked my belief system, describe women's ultimate freedom in fierce anger and retaliation against "spiritual acceptance" and humility, women's burdens for centuries. Believing that traditional Christian notions of femininity have crippled women, Heilbrun cheers Adrienne Rich for vowing to "save the world by doing it for ourselves," and Anne Sexton and Lois Ames for wearing gold disks that proclaimed "never let the bastards [men] win."[1] In describing Dorothy Sayers' life, Heilbrun writes that Sayers, a scholar and talented novelist, eventually moved into "that 'other work,' the study of Christianity," but that "it was in her sinfulness, rather than in her devoutness, that her true destiny as a woman is revealed."[2]

How can a woman call herself a feminist if she buys into Christian values, I wondered. How can one embrace "spiritual acceptance," humility, and forgiveness while stoking up rage for self-empowerment? I felt an uncomfortable degree of sympathy for Heilbrun's argument that women have lost touch with their true selves in their attempt to fit a patriarchal mold, and I worried that I had been socialized to accept (and desire) the giving of myself in so many contexts—to marriage, children, and my Christian faith. I knew that the Christian hierarchy of values I aspire to—putting one's self last, forgiving persecutors, turning the other cheek—would be considered by most feminists as unhealthy and socially imposed.

I thought of myself sometimes as a mutant Christian, surrounded on one side by feminist professors whom I respected and on the other by Christian friends and my church community. I did not know in which setting I felt like the bigger imposter—in church, where the minister described the beauty of childlike faith that always trumps the world's "wisdom," or at school, where my spirituality hid dormant in the farthest recesses of my professional persona. I knew of no one else who shared my mixture of beliefs, a brew that many Christians—including most of those who sat next to me in church—would consider tepid.

I fumed when my Disciples of Christ church decided not to accept female applicants for the pastor's position. On a Sunday morning that brought the first snow of the season, a member of the search committee for our new pastor joked from the pulpit, "We're going to have trouble convincing any man to move where it snows in September!" Smugly, I thought to myself that he'd made a blunder my students often make—referring to generalized people in the masculine rather than using a more gender-neutral term. Within a few moments, I came to understand that the speaker was even less politically correct than I had imagined.

"We've decided as a praying body that we will seek a man, not a woman, to be the pastor of our church," he continued. He stuttered a little, his voice gratingly gentle and apologetic. "We believe this is God's will."

A woman in the row ahead of me whispered something into her husband's ear. I wanted badly to know what she said, but she made the only noticeable reaction around me. No one stood up and questioned this decision. No rustle of discomfort proceeded from the pews. The announcements rolled on. Women's prayer group meeting. Donations for the prison ministry being accepted. I thought of an old friend of mine who told me she once walked out of church after hearing a comment on marriage roles with which she disagreed.

I urged myself for a heart-pumping moment to do the same. *Right now,* I thought, *or no one will know what you're protesting.* I did not budge. I spent the rest of the service imagining myself taking the pulpit by force and making a Thomas Jefferson–type speech.

Good morning, I might say, in my best professorial tone. *For my own peace of mind, I have to tell you I do not believe women should be excluded from positions of power in any context, including religion, marriage, and politics. In contradiction to most of you, I also believe that couples should live together before marriage if they want to, and that they should decide without fear of damnation on the matter of sex before matrimony. These freedoms, along with the option of divorce, I see as crucial to women's self-actualization, and in some cases, personal safety. And, also, while I'm getting it all out on the table, I don't really believe that Eve caused the downfall of humanity.*

I felt miserable the remainder of that Sunday, my emotions flip-flopping between anger and guilt. Did anyone else at that service feel the way I did? I doubted it. I kept coming back to the possibility that my congregation possessed a purer form of faith than I did, that they had an insight into God's will that I lacked because of my own stubborn pride—maybe because of my allegiance to my feminist ideals. Something inside my gut refused to agree with this notion.

I admitted to myself for the first time that Sunday that I believe all of these heretical things because I do not view the Bible as a text written by the hand of God, but rather as a text written by men who had experienced God deeply—and a text through which I can also find God. Although I cannot entirely explain away the contradictions, I believe in miracles, life after death, and the divinity of Jesus. I consider scripture the greatest source of wisdom and spiritual direction in my life. I pray a lot, trying to figure out where God stands on these issues, trying to determine whether my "create your own" approach to spirituality sets me apart from the one thing I want most in the world—a close relationship with God.

I find myself adopting a kind of split personality, reserving the Christian side of myself for limited audiences. Even when a golden opportunity to defend Christianity arises among colleagues, after a bitter comment or joke, I remain silent. I worry about what my colleagues in the English department will think if I pipe up and try to defend a faith that I often hear labeled as ridiculous and oppressive. I sometimes hear caustic remarks about the Inquisition, the Crusades, multiple abuses of women's rights in the name of Christianity, and most recently, following the brutal murder of a gay student at our university, the hate-filled campaigning of Reverend Phelps, who made it his life's work to proclaim that the gay victim was burning in hell for his homosexuality.

I do not balk at the idea that someone in the department will find out about my faith through other means, but to openly preach the good news to individuals who view most Christians as antifeminist fundamentalists? I cannot imagine a greater blow to my roles as feminist and teacher.

About two years ago, a Christian friend offered to help me paint my apartment, and we spent the afternoon rolling ivory tusk paint and talking about spirituality. I remember feeling for much of the day a sense of great comfort and relief to be talking about my beliefs openly, to share with someone who understands my incredible sense of humility and awe at experiencing God. Somehow—I'm sure it was inevitable—we got on the subject of unbelievers and what causes them to shut the door on a spiritual life. "My sister is an atheist," my friend said, "and it breaks my mom's heart." I told her I was sorry. "Well," my friend continued, "my sister got her Ph.D. and that pretty much did it. She decided she was a feminist, and it's like she got too smart to believe in God. My mom prays for her every day."

At those words, the comfort I had been reveling in evaporated, and the room might as well have cracked in half with the division I suddenly felt between my friend and me. I did not respond, but I thought about the sister, and I empathized with her. My friend considered her sister an outsider, and even though I had never met her, I felt at that moment closer to her than my friend who innocently continued taping molding. It was as if the sister and I shared a secret understanding of a well-known fact. Academia holds little tolerance for Christians. Many Christian faiths hold little tolerance for feminism.

God, I prayed for the umpteenth time after the painting episode, *how can something I feel so strongly in my mind and my heart be wrong? What am I supposed to believe?* I opened my Bible to 1 Corinthians and wrote down these two passages, the first on which my eyes fell: "My speech and my proclamation were not with plausible words of wisdom, but with a demonstration of the Spirit and of power, so that your faith might rest not on human wisdom but on the power of God" (2:4–5) and "What no eye has seen, nor ear heard, nor the human heart conceived, what God has prepared for those who love him" (2:9).

Today, I still have not come entirely to terms with my split personality. As knowledge of my Christian faith leaks in various ways to my peers, I feel less and less nervous about their reaction. Maybe, I think, it will prompt them to question simply: how could a woman who considers herself a feminist also be a Christian? How could someone who knows and condemns all of the evils Christians have committed in the name of God still devote herself to Christian beliefs? In the face of my frozen reaction to sharing my faith without prompting, these questions are, right now, the most meaningful witness I can offer. I am far from holding an ideal reconciliation of Christian doctrine and feminist ideals. Like spirituality, I find these reconciliations are personal, and at their best, faith-building. In prayer, when I am not preoccupied with my dueling personas and the many ways I am disappointing my Christian community and my feminist role models, I find the most whole joy I have ever known, a pure brand of peace that reduces me to a blubbering, grateful mess. In these moments of prayer, I reach a tentative reconciliation with my seemingly competing values by doing the most feminist—and the most Christian—thing I can think to do. I lay my struggle in Jesus' lap, and together we tend to it.

Two

For Love of God and Anarchy

Ann Crews Melton

*T*he Texas air hung in a humid blanket as I squished up the hill wrapped in a beach towel, trying not to slap mosquitoes (they're God's creatures too) or trip in my squeaky flip-flops. This was my last year at Pine Cove, a Christian camp hyped up on water-skis and ropes courses, and we had ended a long day by singing to Jesus around a campfire. A male counselor delivered the evening's message, as women were not allowed to speak to the entire group.

Later that night we had "the sex talk" in our cabin, and my counselor—a hip evangelical just a few years older than me—offered her editorial on Paul's pronouncements, advised that we write love letters to our future husbands, and ended by confiding in us that once we were married, we had to fulfill our husbands' needs—especially sexually. Oral sex was okay, if that's what he wanted, and we should offer our bodies any time he felt desire.

It wasn't until I was sitting in a women's studies class a few years later that I realized my camp counselor had justified rape inside of marriage. By this time, I was enduring the clichéd college experience of watching my faith crumble around my progressively hairy ankles, and the sullen void of losing my evangelical Christian identity became interlaced with rage against those who had seemingly brainwashed me and those who justified abuse despite whatever well-meaning intentions.

I grew up in a small country church founded by my Presbyterian ancestors. Although I rarely missed a Sunday, fanatic ecumenism during high school led me to spend Sunday nights at an Assemblies of God church and Wednesdays with an Episcopal youth group. I devoured C. S. Lewis, listened to Christian punk and hard-core, and made a point of arguing at every available opportunity with my artsy, atheist-prone friends. I ended one short-lived relationship because I wasn't confident the guy in question would be joining me in heaven, and I went to a secular college only hoping I could convert more people. Although I had written a play in third grade about women's suffrage and was one of three political "liberals" in my high school government class, I didn't sense the contradiction in my conservative theology and burgeoning politics. Jesus was the answer, and my future was in him.

At college, my Christian bubble exploded. I learned Buddha said similar things as Jesus had, though centuries earlier; I had more fun with the multipierced, purple-haired bisexuals than the guitar-strumming InterVarsity kids; and for the first time I heard the phrase "social justice." After weeks of walking around campus in the wee hours of the morning and sitting distraught in the chapel, I wrote a letter to god and quit going to church.[1] I particularly resented women's marginalization in the communities of my youth and sought out other forms of feminine spirituality for comfort. I cried out to Kali, wrote papers on female Buddhas who walked on water, and participated in Unitarian goddess rituals.

However, as god dragged my new vegan boots grudgingly through the ambiguities of faith, a semester in England turned me on to Julian of Norwich, and a month in India left me crying before a statue of the Blessed Virgin. I couldn't escape Christianity no matter how far I fled. Feminist theology offered moments of solace, but I was still unsettled with the church of my ancestors. There had to be something more than simply leaving the church or learning to reclaim a male Jesus as Wisdom. I fell into a new void, without faith or a firm identity, but would soon tear the darkness that enshrouded me to raise a fist and fashion a black flag.

My study in England was also the first time I met an anarchafeminist. Lisa wore spikes and a black miniskirt to class, showed me how to make tofu bacon, and spouted a more articulate critique of religion than my postmodern biblical history professor. She was an American, but we hung out with an assortment of British socialists and anarchists, many of them queer, and I protested the U.S. government for the first time on the streets of London. I hesitated to join my friends when they went out on midnight spray painting ventures and knew several had been arrested for destroying fields of genetically modified crops. But their passion and love were intense, and I returned to the States intrigued by how to incorporate such passion back into my beliefs, standing against powers set to crush the human spirit and marginalize the immigrants, the Palestinians, the children of Afghanistan, the Hispanic women who cleaned my parents' house, and the African American women who plucked my grandmother's chickens.

Soon after in a feminist theory class, I found one essay buried in our textbook—"Anarchism and Feminism" by Kathryn

Pyne Addelson, Martha Ackelsberg, and Shawn Pyne.[2] The essay wasn't covered in our syllabus, but I delved in and found an articulation of what I already believed. Anarchafeminism is communal in orientation, maintaining that individuals are most free existing in a society of mutual relationships, and likewise, society benefits most when composed of liberated individuals acting cooperatively. Thus anarchy becomes neither nihilism nor rampant chaos, but recognition that we are already part of an interdependent whole—including children, animals, and the ecosystem—and we must share responsibility for new methods of organization without hierarchy or dominance-oppression power systems. Communal anarchy works toward nonhierarchical structure, with locally determined organization of shared leadership, fluidity of roles, and bottom-up decision making. Authority is decentralized such that each community makes decisions by prioritizing its own needs and then networks with other communities addressing similar issues. The whole idea takes a lot of individual initiative and thought, but such constructive alternatives (through food co-ops, free libraries, rape crisis centers, collectively run radio stations) do exist and will continue to enact this process until the dominant system becomes superfluous.

Identifying as an anarchist posed significant problems for my faith. I hoped to be a voice of radical change within the community that raised me and did not want to abandon Christianity, since organized religion will continue to exist in some form regardless of my participation. Rather, I want to push Christianity toward the potential I believe is there, buried deep under the institutions, papal authority, televised madness, and the obnoxious attitude of the Christian right. The more I thought about it, the more my anarchafeminist vision looked like the realm of god where the lion lies down with the lamb. Although I'm not confident this will ever happen, it's the only hope I have left. And in a sense, just like the anarchist co-ops, the realm of god is already happening here and now, in the present moment, every time someone offers water to migrants in the Sonoran desert or an abused woman begins a new life. Rather than despair, we learn to accept the bad with the good, the sordid with the beautiful, and to fulfill our responsibility toward others by striving for peace and envisioning a community made whole.

❁

My religion professors were quite gracious my senior year, allowing me to write a thesis syncretizing an anarchafeminist theology. I studied anarchafeminism, with its roots in Emma Goldman, Peter Kropotkin, and Michael Bakunin, and argued that though they found "faith" primarily in anarchism and denounced the Christian God, there is still room in such an autonomous philosophy for every person to make up her or his own mind regarding spirituality and belief in the divine. I did discover that a couple of people, namely Jacques Ellul and Leo Tolstoy, have attempted to combine Christianity and anarchy before—but at the same time, no one had incorporated feminism or the need to challenge male dominance in every sphere of society, from the church to anarchist philosophy.

Through this theology, I attempted to redefine god as immanent, as around and within while still beyond us, and as part of our ecosystem that deserves respect rather than worship. I wrote a chapter on animal theology, using Andrew Linzey and Stephen Webb, concluding that communion is the ultimate vegan meal since the sacrament offers sustenance and inclusivity without suffering, defying social norms. My vision closed by incorporating freethinkers Hannah Arendt, Elisabeth Schussler Fiorenza, and Cornel West. Looking back I'm still excited by the potential of a new theology derived from communal praxis, although I realize a lot of the theoretical language is self-referential. As I mature and allow my philosophy to evolve, I hope to live into these ideals such that I can better articulate a nonhierarchical existence and faith through experiential references interwoven with academic grounding.

In a few instances, I've been able to test my anarchistic ideology in spiritual circles. Toward the end of college, I met some hip feminists in the National Network of Presbyterian College Women (NNPCW) who gave me a community with space for thought and doubt, as well as embodied spirituality. This community became god for me, as I began to see the capacity for being Christ-like within each of us and the love that arises within a truly welcoming space. While we were painfully criticized by the larger church for "not believing in Jesus and encouraging lesbianism," we took such critique as a challenge to prove that being Christian and feminist is not only possible but also radically inclusive and truer to Christ's diverse body. I talked openly about anarchafeminism and could wholeheartedly endorse the organization of NNPCW, with shared leadership, frequently rotating committee participation, and a decentralized network of women—juxtaposed to the corporate hierarchy the larger denomination had become.

Graduation approached, and I struggled with how to prove my independence while testing my newly formed beliefs. Thesis in hand, lip piercing healed over, and hair back to original color, I sought a job. And what makes more sense for an anarchafeminist than to apply for work at the corporate headquarters of a large religious institution? Embracing the irony of my existence, I soon found myself employed by the Office of Women's Advocacy at the Presbyterian Church (USA) national offices. It offered a position through which I could research emerging women's issues, edit a newsletter, and maintain a resource library, not to mention get paid for raising a ruckus. Our office is uniquely mandated to advocate to the church on behalf of women and to encourage the church to be a "prophetic" voice in society. At my interview I was also assured that our office was run nonhierarchically in spite of the larger institution, so I jumped in with both feet.

Unfortunately, landing flat-footed in newly acquired dress shoes does little to build stamina. I soon found myself buried in an environment of petty power plays and passive-aggressive interactions, not to mention carrying enough work for three associates on my narrow shoulders. Our staff shrinks every year with budget cuts and layoffs, while executive salaries remain in the six-digit range. Add that to the posh boardrooms, an ultramodern chapel, and sterile cubicle space, and you'll find a "church corporation" with dwindling membership and funds struggling to justify existence. It's not easy to watch the institution implode from within, especially when you discover good people sandwiched between layers of bureaucracy and mission work plans. My only hope for the church is to trust the movement of the Spirit to inspire people to destabilize the institution and revision the national offices as a place to network and resource rather than direct and dictate. We must open a place for a new structure and system, and I am empowered by Jesus' table-turning rage to begin clearing that space.

When people inquire about my job, they often comment, "How nice to be doing something meaningful." Some days I nod wearily in response, others I immediately counter with frustrations about the institution that really stem from my discomfort with myself, easily gliding through doors of privilege that will never exist for most people. Occasionally I come into direct contact with my constituents, like meeting two young women from Bangladesh who work in a sweatshop for Wal-Mart. They conveyed their stories with the help of a translator, but mostly through their sad, tired eyes. Such instances remind me why I must struggle, and I silently vow a rigid stance against consumerism. Then I return to my desk, where I sit at my computer, read distant articles about other women in similar circumstances, compile summaries of church policy, and while away time with interludes of e-mail and office chatter. As much as I try to live up to my own inane standards of morality and personal betterment,

I am complicit in the systems that control these women. I cannot promise them things will get better, and on such days I am not sure my faith tradition can offer new life to those facing economic disparity, constant violence, and degradation.

My spiritual life has been squelched while my identity becomes wrapped up in "church as work," so I spend Sundays helping out with Food Not Bombs, sharing vegetarian meals with working-class folk and anarchist kids in a park downtown. I like to think that is where Jesus would be. I understand why it is important for some people to gather around an altar and sing hymns of praise, but my community of faith exists outside the walls of privilege and sanctioned theology. I believe in the Christ-potential in all of us, the ability to actualize divine love and reject an idolatrous God confined to one person in history or a single institution of the present. By decentralizing our faith into the hearts of each one of us, we deepen our capacity to share joy and sadness, allowing god's tears to flow down the cheeks of the marginalized and sustain an ever-flowing stream.

Anarchy has taught me to reject systems of power, and, through my experience, I'm no longer sure god is omnipotent. So I'm fighting the system from within, attempting to embrace the uncertainty of both a god who may not be in control and the impending decision to leave my job for a less secure, but probably equally privileged, freedom. I've been blessed to find work following my passion, but I fear succumbing to the status quo, not to mention burning out by the time I'm twenty-five. Thus I'm paring down my possessions, guarding against that nascent descent into yuppiedom, and looking for opportunities to venture out and live by faith. Through anarchafeminism, where I have a place to define myself, and through Christianity, where I have a place to connect to something larger than myself, I draw strength for the journey. And the journey, the movement by struggle, indeed, may perhaps be the resurrection of us all.

Three

W H A T ' S   I N   A   N A M E ?

Megan Buron Gavin

I have always loved my name. My first, middle, and last name each has five letters and ends with an "n." It's even and balanced, very Irish, too. I take names seriously and believe that a name can shape a person. Therefore, I had a particularly difficult time when choosing a name for the sacrament of confirmation. A confirmation saint is supposed to provide direction in life and an identity in the church. However, most thirteen-year-olds pick pretty names or names that run in the family. Even though I found the names ugly, I decided to choose between my favorite saints: Joan of Arc and Bernadette.

I admired Joan because she rejected the traditional role of women. She dressed as a man and led an army into battle. She fought for her ideals and died rather than abandon her beliefs. In contrast, Bernadette was a pious and sickly young nun. She is remembered because the Virgin Mary appeared to her and instructed her to dig a well. Bernadette, ever obedient, did as she was told despite an illness that made her almost too weak to lift handfuls of dirt. Her will proved strong, and she dug until her fingers bled and water sprang from the ground. Water has flowed from this spot ever since, creating the fountains of Lourdes, where the ailing have sought miracles for centuries. Years ago, when my grandmother was dying of cancer, she visited Lourdes and brought back a bottle of holy water for me. Although the water has long since evaporated and Bernadette's cures were unsuccessful, the bottle remains a precious memory of my Grandma Helen. It was nearly impossible to choose between Joan's strength and defiance and Bernadette's mental stamina and her acceptance of her health and fate.

❁

As a child, I was always cooperative getting ready for church each Sunday. While my three younger siblings begged to sleep for "ten more minutes," I had finished my cereal and was brushing my hair. I looked forward to the weekly opportunity to wear dresses, tights, and nice shoes. I especially loved to sing, and the music shaped my understanding of faith. I knew God as an omnipresent force of protection and benevolence as we sang the words, "Yahweh, I know you are near, standing always at my side. You guard me from the foe and you keep me in ways, everlasting." One of my favorite songs, *We Are the Family,* reminded me of my grandparents, who died when I was little. They personified the words "in our family all are welcome, doesn't matter who you are. In our home there's always room, so plan to stay." Famous for their hospitality, my grandparents welcomed everyone to their table; any friend of a friend was considered family. I sang the refrain as a reiteration of my own beliefs: "We are the family and we are the home, we are the mountain where love can be known, we are the voices and we are the hands for bringing peace to our lands."

My musical tastes did extend beyond the religious. Some of my fondest memories of childhood involved shimmying away to the chords of *Free to Be You and Me,* an album I wore out on my blue and brown Fischer Price record player. I danced to lyrics telling me that boys can play with dolls, girls don't have to be "ladies," moms can fix cars, and dads can cook. I loved the story about the princess, Atalanta, who could run faster than men and earned herself the right to choose if and whom she would marry. She traveled the world having adventures and lived a life of her own choosing. Marlo Thomas and Alan Alda were preaching to an eight-year-old member of their choir.

Along with weekly mass, I attended a Catholic grade school. In fifth grade religion we studied "family life," which is Catholic for sex education. I distinctly remember my teacher turning crimson as she drew nondescript, awkward chalk diagrams of the male and female sexual organs on the board. She explained that a woman's reproductive organs are inside her body because God wants her to stay inside the home to care for her children and husband. The male organs are outside his body because he belongs outside the home working to support his family. When I came home from school that day, I swore in front of my mom for the first time. "Who the hell does she think she is? She left the house to go to work. What a liar!" Even at eleven, I had big plans. I was going to see the world, meet new people, and have adventures just like Atalanta. I didn't plan on staying inside my home, regardless of the location of my ovaries.

Unlike other parishes in the neighborhood, mine did not allow girls to be altar servers. Every year on a sunny, spring day, the altar boys would get the day off of school to have a big picnic. I could not accept that all the girls were supposed to sit in class while the boys were off playing baseball and eating hot dogs. So, as an eighth grader, I planned a walkout for altar boy picnic day. I got other girls to sign a petition indicating our reasons for protest and that our parents knew what we had planned. Of course, my mom didn't just know about it; she thought it was a great idea. Unfortunately, my teachers learned about the walkout beforehand. To appease the situation, they allowed us to spend part of the day playing kickball. They ordered pizzas for lunch, and we ate ice cream in the afternoon. In the end, it was a compromise that wasn't fully satisfying, as I was unable to solve an underlying problem: my church's narrow interpretation of gender.

The rigid definitions of gender so present at school and church were pleasantly blurred in my family. When my cousin Eric was born, my family visited baby and parents in the hospital. At thirteen, I felt particularly sensitive to the unfairness of the birth process. I couldn't get over how wrong it seemed that women go through all the pain while men do nothing. During our visit, my aunt Colleen told me that my uncle John always insisted on giving each of his children their first bath. When the nurses tried to shoo him away, they met with a determined man who wouldn't hear otherwise. He desperately wanted to wash his messy little babies as they screamed. I didn't reflect much on the story at the time, but I realize now that John sensed unfairness, too. He wanted the closeness that seems effortless between mother and child. In the absence of that physical intimacy, he found ways to be close to his children. When his daughter, Helen, fell and scraped her knee, she would run crying to her dad. He could soothe her better than anyone else. He, like the other men in my family, applied band-aids, helped with homework, and cried at weddings. In my family, emotional complexity and parenting do not belong to one sex.

I also learned a good deal about Catholicism from my elder relatives. Two of my great-uncles were Christian Brothers who each spent thirty years teaching in Nicaragua. They introduced me to the life of Bishop Oscar Romero, who fought against an oppressive government during the U.S.-funded war in El

Salvador. "I fed the poor, and they called me a saint. I asked why they were poor, and they called me a communist," Romero said before he was assassinated.

The Christian Brothers founded my high school, so it also exhibited a commitment to serving the poor. Yearly religion class and community service were graduation requirements. We all spent time at soup kitchens, organizing clothing drives, or tutoring children who lived in subsidized housing. However, I found many contradictions to this humanitarian perspective. While members of Amnesty International discussed human rights abuses in Latin America, students in JROTC (the U.S. Army's Junior Reserve Officers' Training Corps) held rifle practice in the school basement. Rita Mae Brown and James Baldwin, gay literature favorites, were required reading, but the school would not support the creation of a gay and lesbian student group. While both male and female students had to wear the infamous Catholic school uniforms, the dress code and its enforcement revealed the school's attitude towards women. The girls wore a black and white pleated jumper and white knee-high socks. When feeling rebellious, we could tie black sweaters around our waists or wear gray tights. If we showed up in pants on a subzero Minnesota morning, the administration would slap detentions on us for covering our legs or "being out of uniform." Yet, wearing skirts too far above the knee warranted detentions, too. The margin of acceptable behavior for women was insultingly narrow.

❖

When college shopping, I had one nonnegotiable requirement— not Catholic. I was thrilled that my freshman year roommates at Boston University were Jamaican and Jewish women. I accompanied the latter to High Holiday services at the start of the semester. As we rocked back and forth hitting our hands against our chests, I understood no Hebrew but unintentionally began to mutter *"mea culpa"* under my breath. Apparently guilt is not a Catholic invention. I met other Jewish students at school and became a bit jealous of a friend when I heard her rabbi at home was a lesbian. I went to mass only on Ash Wednesdays, and the rest of the time I attended Protestant services on campus with my two best friends, a Lutheran and a Methodist. The choir was fantastic, but the congregation rarely sang and the hymns were unfamiliar. The assistant pastor was even a woman, but the church was bare, there was precious little stained glass, and the congregation only spoke to pray the "Our Father." It reminded me of going to a lecture.

A few years later, I lived in Brookline, Massachusetts, a town with a large Orthodox Jewish community. I watched as little girls in long skirts followed their mothers, who also wore skirts and always covered their heads by wearing scarves or wigs. The next year I lived in West Africa and observed many Muslim women following this same practice. In Niger, I had some female friends who wore veils and some who did not. I knew men with three wives and others with one. I read parts of the Qur'an and books by a Moroccan feminist writer, Fatima Mernissi. One day I sat on my host sister's bed, leafing through a book of famous quotations. My host mother came across Gloria Steinem's "a woman without a man is like a fish without a bicycle." I watched as the words and meaning came together and a pensive look fell over her face. She asked me, "Can a woman ever really be happy without a man?" I smiled to myself as I realized how much my wonderful Muslim host mother resembled my Catholic fifth grade teacher. "They are all the same," I thought, "all of them, different only in degrees." At that point, I knew Christian, Jewish, and Muslim men and women and had some small appreciation for the variety of thought within each religion. Yet, the thread of patriarchy connecting all three left me to wonder: if I was going to leave Catholicism for its misogyny, where was I to turn?

❁

Certainly my mother's daughter, I was a feminist long before I could quote Gloria Steinem, long before I read *The Feminine Mystique*.[1] My mom is the head of the household, has always worked and made sacrifices for her family. She integrates her values in her professional life by teaching fourth graders from a book called *Herstory*, assigning homework on civil rights leaders, and urging her students to question why some people are homeless and others live in excess. My mother is also a phenomenal cook, throws excellent parties, and knows how to cure fevers and heartache. She's intelligent, strong, and passionate. Because of her, I grew up understanding feminism as complementary to family and domestic happiness. My feminism recognizes that parenthood, family, and other womanly traits do not contradict its ideals. As a feminist, I don't have to reconcile Joan and Bernadette; I have all the elements of my identity intact. I find it disappointing that I don't have this as a Catholic. The church does not allow me to combine the elements of my identity that I saw (or hoped to see) in my two saints: strength and defiance along with acceptance and quiet resolve.

❁

My good friend, who is preparing for ordination in the United Methodist Church, asked recently where it was that the Catholics lost me. I wonder that myself. I don't go to mass anymore, except when I'm home for the holidays. For the past two years my most meaningful faith experiences have occurred while celebrating Passover with my boyfriend's family. I was surprised to learn that Passover is a holiday that never involves going to synagogue. At first, I found it odd to celebrate an entire religious ceremony from one's own dining room table. I began to appreciate the value in this private celebration as I observed the thoughtful preparations, from the selection of prayers and songs to the menu and its spiritual implications. The good china comes out; so does the seder plate, Isaiah's wine glass, and the prayer books. We read Psalms and discuss their meaning. The youngest at the table explains "why this night is different from other nights." There's something about the glow of candlelight bouncing off wine glasses, the gold and cream Havilland and the cobalt blue of the tablecloth that is oddly reminiscent of stained glass. Time is suspended as the guests share food, prayers, and ideas. The room is transformed into a place of worship, and those at the table create and define the holy space. I enjoy the intimacy and honesty of a religious celebration free from a man in a robe acting as the conductor of my spiritual life. Here at this table I am nourished instead of compromised. Only God is watching.

The tranquility I appreciate at Passover reminds me of midnight mass on Christmas Eve. The congregation is silent for thirty minutes before mass begins. The choir sings softly, accompanied by violins and candlelight and falling snow. The church is filled, yet no one speaks, hardly a cough, barely a sneeze. It's the only hour and a half of the entire year when the church is totally calm. Everyone sits patiently in their cranberry and pine colors, children closing their eyes, couples leaning against one another, kissing on the cheek. On this night, at this hour, the meals have been cooked, and the presents are wrapped. For this hour there is rest. At night, in the dark, the cold, and the quiet, God comes more readily. We've made more space for such a presence. Throughout the mass the music rises, the anticipation builds, the trumpets announce the crescendo, and mass ends sending us with warm hearts into the cold night.

❖

Two weeks before confirmation I had to tell the priest my confirmation name. I had come to the realization that I couldn't choose between the two. I needed Joan because I aspired to be independent, courageous, and passionate, and to follow my own dreams. But I wasn't complete with Joan because she had to dress like a man, bind her breasts, and cut her hair. I needed Bernadette not only because she kept me grounded and connected to my roots, but also because she represented my femininity, my stamina, and my willingness to accept hardship. So I told the priest that I was taking two names. He was surprised but accepted my choice and confirmed me Bernadette Joan.

In this case the church allowed me the names I wanted; yet, the church has never allowed me the identity that the names represent. This is, perhaps, why I am most comfortable and more able to pray where there is no conflict, where I don't feel compromised. I have tried to call myself a feminist and a Catholic, and it's a challenge that demands continuous self-reflection and compromise. But the church makes no compromise in return. I want to believe that my family's Catholicism is still possible. But the church is steadfast and moving in the opposite direction. Of the many names I have that shape and inform my identity, I wonder if *Catholic* has become an incongruous term, a name that no longer fits?

Four

EMBRACING YOUR BEAUTY, MOVING IN STRENGTH

Heather Scheiwe

y childhood was filled with beauty. The majesty of coarse, purple granite mountains that sprouted from the rich, red soil of the Colorado prairie did not intimidate me. Rather, I grew lean and strong from scrambling up the rock inclines and twisted pine trees that surrounded my home. I tossed aside the plastic birthday Barbie I received in favor of feeling the grain of wooden planks between my palms as I hammered together birdfeeders, stools, forts. My fingers were often tinged not with my mother's stolen lipstick, but with blackberry juice from the wild vines crawling along the backyard fence. It was a time of pure faith in the goodness of God, the world, and myself, but in the midst of my adventurous childhood, I learned that this sort of independent beauty was not the beauty I ought to possess.

My experience and thus my impression of what was beautiful sharply distinguished me from Girl—that slender, popular, eyelash-batting image of beauty that most girls my age were striving to attain. Comments about how "cute" I was because of my petite frame sent me running to the soccer fields to prove otherwise. There I would match my steps with the boys as I let my tangled hair fly unbraided. While other girls were asked to "go out" by male classmates, I was writing stories about adventures I longed to have outside the walls of the classroom. I did not, would not, enact the role people expected from my external appearance.

My faith was the only strength I possessed that was socially acceptable for a girl, so I immersed myself in Christian activities, soon becoming a leader in ministries both at church and at school. It frustrated me that other girls my age were not interested in the deeper issues of faith, and I felt very alone. Yet, I questioned confirmation teachers about their theology, met with administrators to gain the right to pray around the school's flagpole, wrote curriculum for youth groups, and gave testimonies in front of hundreds. While most people in this sector affirmed and used my unique ability to "get the job done," I heard from them another definition of Girl. Pastors, teachers, and peers promised that if we good Christian girls continued in a quiet life of service and submission, God would construct the perfect man to reward and rescue us. Although this definition had little to do with fashion trends or physical relations with boys, as the definition of the secular Girl had, I still did not fit the mold of woman that my learned Christianity had constructed. Although I tried to live with the integrity of Christ, was I too strong, too bold, too risky, and too intimidating to be calling myself a "woman of God"?

Every youth conference I attended alleged that the only acceptable way to grow spiritually is to sacrifice your pride. One night in particular, engulfed in the booming bass of the praise band and the flashing colors of the strobe light, the preacher called for us to give up all our needs, all our desires, all we were, for they were not in line with the will of God. "Your sin is your self. Lay it down on the altar of sacrifice. This alone is holy and pleasing to the Lord!" he commanded from the stage. So I raised my hands in desperation to God, expecting to feel released from the burden of my personal strength and independence that seemed so at odds with the way a Christian woman should be.

Rather than an overall sense of peace, however, my wrists felt as though weights were shackled to them. I thought this heaviness was God giving me a physical manifestation of the blatant pride I had exhibited since childhood. My arms dropped to my sides as I opened my eyes to the roar around me. People were swaying and weeping and crying out to God for forgiveness. But I felt nothing but the burden of my strong personality bearing down on me like one of the granite rocks I used to climb. I was a stranger in a strange land, and I thought it was my fault.

I wanted so desperately to live a life of consistency, to find an exterior manifestation for my interior desire to lose myself for the sake of Christ. Serving others was such an abstract concept, but I thought that by sacrificing my personal time and desires, I would be more aligned with God's will. I gave away half my clothing, committed myself never to date again, and packed every spare moment with volunteer work. Ironically, this kind of behavior was rewarded with public recognition, scholarships, and more requests for my services. I tried desperately to make everyone happy, to meet everyone's needs, but I could never give enough to alleviate my conscience. This overwhelming ambition led me down a path that was not only destructive to my understandings of God and myself, but one that almost took my very life.

❋

I convinced myself I did not need food. Children with sunken eyes and pocked skin cried out for bread from the TV screen, and I wept because I was eating an unnecessary cookie. *Too many peo-*

ple go hungry every day for me to gorge myself on the fat of the land, I thought. I should be using my time to do God's will, to serve others. As a Christian accustomed to the discipline of daily Bible reading, I was determined to be disciplined with my food intake, too. I monitored when I grew hungry and trained myself to wait a bit longer before eating. Then I cut out anything that did not provide some nutrient necessary for healthy body functions: no unnatural sugar, no white flour, no carbohydrates when I could choose vegetables, no dairy products since I could take calcium supplements. I trained myself to feel guilty with every bite, knowing I did not "need" it to get through the day. It was purely selfish to consume more than what I absolutely needed to survive.

I ran for miles on an empty stomach and pumped my arms furiously, like a machine with dumbbells attached, demanding that my body pay for its own greedy sins. I maximized every moment of time, flexing and releasing muscles while in class, walking outside even in air that pocked my skin with red burns from the cold. I filled my belly with coffee until it stung from the acid. The pain gave me an excuse not to eat, to transcend all those evil things of the world: need, time, desire. I just wanted to be assured of something about myself and know, *feel*, that it was real. I was seeking definition, but the only thing clearly defined in my life, in myself, were my muscles. My arms and legs were sinewy cords that flexed with every movement. Clothes fit so loosely, there was no doubt my body contained no excess. I reveled in the tightness of my body, delighted in this exhibition of my strong character. Finally, people would not confuse me with one of "those girls," the demure, petite, passive girls who pervaded both magazine covers and church pews.

❖

Twenty pounds lost and two hospitalizations later, it was obvious my external strength wasn't resolving my personality confusion. In fact, only one defining factor came out of those two years of intense concentration—I had developed anorexia. I wanted to rid myself of all selfishness, yet I also wanted to distinguish myself from feminine stereotypes I did not fit emotionally, spiritually, or relationally. I was trying to conform to the mold of the Christian woman, as I understood it, while also struggling to break it. I wanted healing so desperately, but at that time, merely as a means to proclaim that God's strength had won out over my weakness. How humble I was.

The only way I knew how to express my deep desire for healing was by sublimating it in service to others. I read multiple perspectives on the roots of eating disorders, wrote research papers on fasting nuns in medieval times, and even started a prayer group for young women on campus. My brain never allowed the subject to rest, but I never allowed it to touch my own personal experience, either. As long as my work was benefiting other people, my time and effort spent on the subject were legitimized. But the experts' solutions didn't address my issues. My problems had little to do with how much I read fashion magazines (rarely, if ever), how desperately I wanted guys to like me (boyfriends? too much trouble!), or how thin I wanted to be (I wanted to be strong, not skinny). As much as God's grace kept me alive, I still didn't have answers that went beyond the body, answers that touched the Spirit of truth.

That same semester, I began therapy and I enrolled in my first women's studies class. Recognizing my curiosity and academic determination, a professor encouraged me to take his course, Christian Theology and Human Existence. I knew this professor taught Feminist Theology as well—a course I distinctly remember telling him I had no interest in taking because I thought feminism was too radical to integrate with Christian faith—but I figured this course was free of any indoctrinating feminist dogma. God bless the professor's compassionate, persistent heart. He knew that class was exactly what I needed. In the first book we read, Reinhold Niebuhr discussed not one, but *two* facets of sin: pride, defined as thinking one deserves more than one actually does, and sensuality, defined as thinking one is not worthy of anything more than basic, physical realities of human existence.

That was it.

For years, all I had heard was that we were a bunch of self-centered, ungrateful creatures. To reconcile ourselves to God, we needed to repent of our pride and give ourselves completely to the service of God and others. But that narrow solution was my—and many other women's—very stumbling block. While our religion had told us to continually "give ourselves to God," we remained empty-handed, without a self to give. Pride was not our problem. We didn't think well enough of ourselves in the first place, so we tried to define ourselves by caring for others and waiting for the perfect man. In seeking to rid myself of pride, I had succumbed to a sense of unworthiness that was just as contrary to the will of God. It was the very faith that claimed to redeem us that kept us in the cycle of spiritual (and near physical) death, rarely allowing us to emerge into the fullness of life Jesus promised. As much as I saw myself differently than most passive women, I was, in practice, weighed down by the very classification I sought to transcend. This new understanding of sin provided a fresh lens through which I could examine my own struggles with self-abnegation, and in turn, identify this same struggle in so many women around me. I remembered the chains I had felt clamp down on my wrists years before, and, no matter how desperately I wanted to know that God was good and I would be okay, I felt like a foreigner in the swirling world of Christian faith once again.

Almost as an act of defiance, I declared myself a women's studies major the spring of my junior year. I also started sharing my story of struggle with anorexia, declaring to others that years of negative messages from men and the male-controlled media had nearly killed me. No more would I be afraid of the word "feminist," for it represented a rich part of life from which Christianity had, without explanation, disconnected me.

"Feminist" provided a definition, one that could hold the weight of my strength without demanding I recant. Yet even though the anorexia was rooted in this very search for definition, I was not healed in finally gaining one. If I wanted to heal, I had to come home to my body, enter into "it" and realize "it" was not just part of me. It was me. And being "feminist" without the unity of my body and my spirit was just another externally dictated label.

❧

In a tenuous attempt to revisit the only place in which I had felt whole—my Christian faith—I applied to a program called the Oregon Extension. Twenty students from top Christian colleges around the country gathered in a small mountain village to take an intensive class called "The Struggle for Self and Voice in Community: Women in Literature and Theology." Our leaders were an egalitarian, middle-aged bohemian couple named Nancy and John. Most of us participants teetered outside the seemingly narrow gate of modern Christianity. Some were exploring other religions, some were trying desperately to reclaim some form of Christianity for themselves, and some were too wounded to trust much of anything. But we came, all of us with at least a mustard seed of faith. There, in the misty woodlands of Oregon, a cloud of witnesses was unveiled to me, a sisterhood of women whose faith and strength were not contrary to one another, but complementary. As we read the sensual poetry of Julian of Norwich, studied the bold initiatives of biblical women, and followed the social revolution of Dorothy Day, I realized that the image I'd understood to be the acceptable Christian woman was actually the very image Jesus shattered every day of his ministry.

Jesus did not pat passive women on the head and urge them to be more subservient—that was the identity their culture dictated to them. Rather, he called women like the one caught in adultery to speak her own forgiveness. He honored women who spent their entire lives giving themselves away with the chance to rest and to gather themselves back in (see John 8:1–11, Luke 10:38–42). In doing so, Jesus affirmed that the historical "woman of God" did not need to shrink from her strong personality, but rather embrace her character as a gift from the Creator. I saw myself reflected in the theories about silence, beauty, and self-abnegation. Slowly, I began to see that a God who brings freedom would not confine me to a way of being simply because I am a certain gender. But I was not yet free.

The community of believers in Oregon, both those present in word and those present in flesh, did not dictate a step-by-step plan as to how I should heal. No one coddled me because I was recovering from an eating disorder. No one tried to counsel me with simple maxims like, "Give it all to God" or "God's power is made perfect in your weakness." We did not play roles of "helper" and "helped." Instead, we were *all* the broken, the healers, the mourners, and the ministers. We learned to name our own pain and allowed ourselves to live in it rather than bandage it with pat explanations and attempts to transcend. Only in opening the wounds and exposing them to find their sources could they begin to heal. This alone was an act of courage.

During that time, we spoke our pain through poetry and dance and music. We learned to use our voices to cry out for the justice and liberation promised to us as children of God, literally climbing to the peak of a mountain one night and screaming, *"Freedom!"* to the golden summer moon. We pounded the wooden floors of our cabins with the sweaty soles of our feet, dancing like wild flames from a desert bonfire. We swam in cool mountain ponds, batting lily pads and laughing at our unorthodox baptism into the new world of ourselves. We celebrated each new day with a homemade treat: brownies gooey with melted fudge, fresh carrots with the tassels still attached, coffee sweet and rich with real cream. Nancy called our mid-morning snack an act of resistance. I called it a part of my salvation. I learned to eat there, because I learned what hunger was—the deep yearning for community, acceptance, and flexibility in definitions: grace. I was being baptized into something I didn't understand. I was coming home.

❉

After that summer, I began to gain weight. Surprisingly, I wasn't even aware that I was eating well and exercising appropriately again. I had quit the structured program and was learning to listen to my own needs. Simple successes marked my days, not in pounds, but in personal choices. I remember the day I walked into the cafeteria, paused in front of the cereal, and poured myself a bowl of chocolate puffs, not because I should nor because everyone else said they were good. I was simply hungry for chocolate puffs, so I ate them in celebration, with thanksgiving, without guilt. It was funny to discover that I really *did* like broccoli, not because some health magazine said I should, nor because I wanted to spite the nutritionist—who insisted I only ate vegetables because I was trying to avoid "getting fat." I was learning to trust my inner voice of love.

My Christian faith gave me a vocabulary to speak about this voice: "When the Spirit of truth comes, he will guide you into all the truth . . ." (John 16:13). I became especially intrigued with the mystics, an independent strain of Christians who dedicated themselves to the holy act of listening deeply as a means to loving God. They seemed to know themselves, and God, so well, and I longed to follow their path. But the very center of their faith—silent contemplation of God—demanded a path uniquely my own. At first, the spiritual practice of meditative prayer terrified me. I remember sitting alone in a cold library chair with only the buzz of halogen lights meeting my silence. I grew anxious by the second, habitually shaking my foot and thinking of all the precious minutes of God's will I was wasting. When I couldn't stand the silence any longer, I glanced impatiently at my watch. Only five minutes had passed.

Slowly, patiently, I had to learn to face myself in the silence. There is a truth I need to hear, not from the instruction of external sources, nor from the audible words of my own story, but by listening deeply, first to my own rushing river of anguish, then to the calm stream whispering beneath. This stream is the living water of the Holy Spirit, crying out to my spirit of God's name for me—Beloved.

❖

Healing is a process of becoming. I live in the already-but-not-yet, knowing that I am not all God has created me to be, but trusting that I am a beautiful child of the God who affirmed all of life by being made flesh. I do not seek to transcend the paradox, but to embrace the tension, for this is where grace, faith, and love reside. *Every* ritual of life has become sacred, not just the events bannered under "Sacrifice." Bathing, dancing, praying, crying, embracing, eating— all have become acts of faith. With every running step, I praise God for the beauty of my curves that protect precious organs inside me. As I celebrate another year of life with friends, I am reminded of the God who uses fire and wind and tears and laughter to touch our hearts. In worship, I experience the glory of Creator God in jewel-colored glass, poetic hymns, and incense that tingles in my lungs.

I cannot doubt that God has blessed me with this feminist path, a path that has only served to invigorate my Christian faith. I believe Jesus' radical call to discipleship includes all people as equals and ushers them into a new way of being—free from societal stigmas and expectations that silenced and shrouded them from using their gifts for the kingdom of God. I could not imagine my Christian faith without integrating my feminist perspective, nor could I practice feminism without integrating Christ's model of equality and compassion and strength. I continue to listen to God's will for fullness in my life, and I trust that I am acting with the integrity that honors *all* of me: leader, writer, speaker, woman, feminist . . . beautiful child of God.

Five

B I R T H   O F   A   M O T H E R   S E L F

MaryAnn McKibben Dana

*I*t's naptime, and my toddler is standing in her crib, wailing into the darkened room. I can tell she's tired, even though she's protesting sleep mightily. Brahms' "Lullaby" waltzes softly through the CD player, an absurd soundtrack for my daughter's foot-stomping fit. None of the usual mommy maneuvers can calm her enough for me to leave the room. She just wants *me*.

I love this child more than life itself, but today is my sermon-writing day. I need to be downstairs, working. I need her asleep and out of my hair for just a little while. I need that, not only because a sermon does not write itself, but also because when I write I feel creative, and authentic, and strangely subversive—like I myself am a toddler in an adult body, stamping my foot and saying "No!" to everything that is oppressive and false in this world. Of all the days for a nap protest, why today?

I imagine a fictional conversation in which I tell her that I love her, but I also love being a pastor, and being a pastor inevitably means being away from her every now and then. I explain that while I understand and appreciate her frustration, I have needs, too. I even talk to her about feminism and how generations of women put their needs dead last for the sake of everyone else, and that's not healthy, so I need her to cooperate just a little bit, for the sake of Mommy's sanity. And I imagine her listening and nodding sympathetically, then lying down and humming herself to sleep while I come downstairs to write in peace.

I laugh at this ridiculous fiction. At twenty months old, she couldn't possibly care less about my needs. Nothing is more important to her than the intensity of these emotions she's feeling. Her inability to deal with frustration and fatigue takes up all the available space in her consciousness. Such is the life of the toddler. And such is the role of the mother. Schedules be damned, I must tend to her, I *will* tend to her. This drama plays out constantly in our house, and in the house of every mother who dares to long for something that is uniquely hers.

Still, I love my daughter's self-centeredness, even as I realize that my needs are important too, and that letting my child eclipse my very existence isn't good for her, let alone me. But what is the alternative? What does feminist mothering look like?

❖

I have been a feminist literally for as long as I can remember, and it was my father who nurtured the impulse in me. He helped me put together my second-grade history fair project, a newspaper patterned after Susan B. Anthony's newspaper, *The Revolution*, which advocated for women's suffrage and an eight-hour workday. Its motto: "Men their rights and nothing more, women their rights and nothing less."

As a high school senior, I was faced with deciding between the academic powerhouse university and the less rigorous local college. Although I was less excited about the latter, I was ready to enroll because it was my boyfriend's choice of school. My father called me one day and laid it all out. "You know where you really want to go," he said. "You know where you will be excited and challenged. And believe me when I say, no man would *ever* sell himself short to be near a woman. Don't you do it either."

Thankfully, I didn't. The high school boyfriend rode alone into the sunset, and I received a superb education at the academic powerhouse.

Where was my mother in all this? She was cleaning, preparing meals, and shuttling the children from place to place. This was not the life she chose after weighing all the options; this was the life she was raised to have. It would take years for me to appreciate the irony of my father encouraging my inner feminist while living in an ultratraditional marriage.

When my parents divorced, I watched my mother take on a variety of new roles: caregiver, yes, but also provider, lawn-care specialist, and repairer of small household mishaps. By then, however, my feminism was on a specific trajectory. Marriage seemed superfluous; children, a nice indulgence for someone else. I was strong, ambitious, determined to venture boldly into the world and change it for the better. As my mother's plucky juggling act gave way to anxiety attacks, I resolved to focus my energies on my career, to live a streamlined life, and to achieve great things for humanity.

The reality is, I had no idea what a feminist spouse and mother would look like. My predivorce mother seemed trapped and unhappy; my postdivorce mother seemed trapped and unhappy with a lot more to do. My feminism didn't have a place for the messy dilemmas that come from weighing the wants and needs of many people. I certainly had no context for understanding the sacrificial nature of motherhood as anything other than a total defeat and loss of self.

But feminism was as intrinsic to my identity as left-handedness or the ability to sing on key. I couldn't have let it go if I'd wanted. So for a long time I let visions of family and motherhood go instead.

✿

If feminism was the irresistible force in my life, then faith was the immovable object—stubborn and huge, lurking in the corner, demanding not to be ignored. I was baptized into the Roman Catholic Church and later raised in a Southern Baptist congregation. Both traditions traded heavily in guilt. I absorbed doctrines of shame and fear that were incompatible with the self-confident feminism that already lived deep in my marrow. I quit the church, and I quit God.

But the hulking presence in the shadows wouldn't budge. I could run, and I could doubt, but I was a Christian; I *am* a Christian. Eventually I found my way to the Presbyterian Church, a denomination that calls both women and men to all ministries of the church—and that affirmed me in my call to ordained ministry. The church laid weighty hands on me and now calls me pastor. In recent years, the irresistible force and the immovable object have collided countless times. Neither is obliterated, or even weakened; rather, the collision always produces an explosive burst of energy.

Feminism and faith commingled for me in a time of spiritual darkness, when I doubted not only God's presence, but also myself. One night I had a dream in which I was sitting on a shady porch. Behind me, a woman slowly and lovingly braided my hair. When I heard her say, "I have knit you together in your mother's womb," I instantly knew it to be true. The God of guilt was no more. Shame, fear, and judgment were no more. I knew that a feminist faith meant that God could be—was!—maternal, powerful, and fierce in her love for all creation.

God as Mother made intuitive sense.

Me as mother still seems an awkward and bewildering prospect.

If feminism, on its own, was inadequate to help me navigate the landscape of motherhood, Christianity was equally unhelpful. Traditional Christian culture paints motherhood as wholesome and inoffensive; the daily ups and downs of childrearing are amusing and adorable, but never heartbreaking, never crippling, and certainly never more than we can bear. Mary, the mother of Jesus and our theological prototype, has been flattened into bland submission. The bloody reality of childbirth goes virtually unspoken; breastfeeding is accepted so long as it is done discreetly and appropriately, preferably out of sight. Images of motherhood are photographed through soft filters—a carnation on Mother's Day, a rose on the communion table to celebrate a birth, benevolent sighs at a child's baptism.

Indeed, for a denomination that baptizes infants, the danger is that baptism becomes the Cute Sacrament, rather than the tectonic shift it truly is. After all, the baptized one is dying and rising right before our eyes. The parents vow to teach their child the Christian faith, but just as important, they deliver their beloved one into the arms of the community, a naked admission of inadequacy for the task of raising a child. No matter how strong we are, no matter how enlightened our views, we simply cannot do it alone. The feminism of strength and autonomy I inherited from my father did not equip me for this surrendering, this confession that I need support. Still, I hand my child over with an additional pleading from deep within my feminist marrow: "Teach her about the God who cherishes femaleness as much as maleness, yet transcends both categories. And please, please, do not ever preach a gospel of shame to my daughter."

Like much of the culture, the church has not adequately affirmed the variety of mothering decisions we make for the good of our children and ourselves. The church has not provided sufficient space for women who've made different choices to talk honestly to one another. Church groups for stay-at-home mothers meet during the day. Mothers working outside the home meet after work, on weekends, or not at all. (Most working mothers feel a desperate need for community, but find it difficult to rationalize the additional time away from their children.) Truth telling is dangerous, particularly across this great divide. Stay-at-home mothers dare not admit to feeling fed up, cornered, or sick of their children, otherwise they have failed at their fundamental biological identity. Working mothers cannot lament how difficult it is to keep the house clean, the kids tended, and their minds on their work—to do so is an admission that women can't survive in the workplace.

My feminism does not inoculate me from these dynamics. I long to be the bold truth-teller I feel my feminist faith has called me to be; in the meantime, I am as mired in these complexities as anyone. I hold my performance up to our culture's two-dimensional rendering of motherhood, and although I recognize it as laughably unrealistic, I still judge myself inadequate. This is the curse of motherhood, even (or perhaps especially) for a feminist—the constant second-guessing, the occasionally debilitating self-doubt. The realities of sleep deprivation and relentless on-the-job parenting training can reduce even the most self-possessed woman to a shrill, paranoid mess.

When people inquire as to our family's child-care situation, I am quick to downplay the amount of time our daughter spends in child care. I emphasize my Fridays off, my relatively short workdays, and my husband's flexible work situation that enables him to care for her when I have evening meetings. Why can't I just say, "She's in day care, she loves it, we cherish our time together, and I am a better mother for it"?

I long for places where women can tell the truth about motherhood. I believe that communities of faith can be such places, and in rare cases, have already begun to be—but only when they embrace the ideals of feminism as well.

While I was pregnant, I was given the gift of a Blessingway, a ritual that focuses not on the impending child, but on the impending mother. It is a rite of passage and a preparation for the travails of labor and the hard work of motherhood. Labor horror stories are forbidden; the emphasis is on affirming the mother-to-be's strength and gifts for motherhood. At its core, the Blessingway is a truth-telling gathering, a means of empowerment, and a deeply creative feminist space.

While the Blessingway has its roots in the Navajo tradition, it can be adapted for a Christian setting. At my Blessingway, a group of treasured women laid hands on me and prayed, strung beads on twin necklaces for the baby and me, and wrote an impromptu lullaby, which I share with my daughter almost daily. It is sung to the tune of "Edelweiss":

Peace of God, peace of God,
May God's comfort surround you;
Peace of God, peace of God,
"Fear not, for I am with you."

God knit together your innermost parts,
She will hold you forever;
Peace of God, peace of God,
Whispering songs forever.

One wise friend sat in the corner and knitted as the evening progressed. I watched her and remembered my dream from so long ago, in which God braided my hair and knit me together, and I knew that my friend's knitting was a prayer and a ritual act for me. Later that evening, she said, "Here is my gift for you. It may not sound like a gift you want. In the gospel of John, Jesus uses an example of a woman forgetting the pains of labor. It is obvious that Jesus never gave birth, because he is wrong. You don't forget. And you shouldn't forget. Labor is profound and powerful. The experience marks your soul. Never forget that.

"Pregnancy will likely leave you with things you wish you could get rid of—stretch marks, extra weight, maybe surgical scars. You may need to be stitched back together after your labor. But never forget, and never take for granted—those things mark you as a mother. Wear those scars with pride. You are strong. And you are marked, as surely as a warrior is marked for battle."

Motherhood is indeed a battle, although it is a battle within oneself. During my childbirth class we were each invited to discern our central question about labor. What was the fundamental root of our anxiety and fear about the process of giving birth? I carried my question around in my journal for months: How do I surrender to the process of giving birth without becoming passive?

I remember this question even today, because it remains my essential struggle as a mother: How do I respond to the needs of my child in the moment, without losing myself?

Good strong feminists are allergic to surrender, I think. It's an embarrassing word, heavy with patriarchal and theological baggage. Control is a precious commodity for us, because for so many years, women didn't have it. But I could not control my labor. I prepared spiritually and physically for it, and then, through some miracle of grace, I let myself be swept along in its wild and unpredictable course. I surrendered, not to the will of the doctors and nurses, but to the process, fraught as it is with mystery. And I connected to a power I didn't know I had.

Now, as a mother, I still struggle with the idea of surrender; the concept still embarrasses me. And yet it is embedded in our Christian tradition, and there is something strangely comforting about it. And so I set my intent: I will surrender, not to rigid and unrealistic expectations, and not to the will of someone else, but I will surrender to the dance of motherhood and to the One who is knitting all the pieces together and who can be trusted in my letting go.

In Search of Integrity

DISCUSSION QUESTIONS

1. Where are you right now in your life in the following categories?

   - Vocationally?
   - Spiritually?
   - Relationally?
   - Recreationally?
   - Politically?
   - Economically?
   - Socially?

2. What challenges do you face in each of these categories that make it difficult to live and act with integrity?
3. What successes have you had in each of these categories of living and acting with integrity?
4. For each of the preceding categories, how has your integrity been challenged or supported by your faith? By your feminism?
5. How has the integrity of your faith challenged your feminism? How has the integrity of your feminism challenged your faith?
6. In what specific experiences in your life has your personal integrity been challenged by societal values and customs?
7. What tensions can you articulate between the demands in your life and your basic set of beliefs? Have you found creative ways to ease those tensions?
8. What role models of integrity do you have in your life? How do these people speak to you of what it means to live an authentic life?
9. What people support you in your struggle to live with integrity? Are there people who make the journey difficult?

10. How have you been successful in crafting an authentic life? How have you had success in blending faith and feminism?

VISIONING ACTIVITIES

Consider the seven categories listed in question 1 and respond to the following:

1. Envision a holistic future that is guided by your faith and feminist values. How would each of these categories look for you as an individual if it were possible to lead a life of complete integrity and authenticity?
2. How might beliefs about each of these categories need to change on a national level to be more supportive of authentic living for everyone in our country? Put another way, what national values need to change to help support people in living more holistic, authentic lives? How could you contribute to this change?

All of us begin with the personal to understand how we fit into our communities. Before you venture into the other sections of this book we invite you to write your story of the search for integrity when holding space in your life for both feminism and faith. Please include your voice in this conversation.

Part Two   **IN SEARCH OF COMMUNITY**

*One glance at our calendars and we know it will be
weeks before we can get together. Claire juggles graduate
school and two jobs. Rachel must carve out small windows
of studio time between freelance and temp employment.
Most of the people we know struggle against the slippery
myth of achieving balance in one's life. Yet we long for
more opportunities to talk about our shared experiences
as young Christian feminists.*

*We feel lucky to have met at all. What serendipity to
find another young woman who claims feminism and was
raised Christian. Where are our peers? In our opinion,
sexism is far from being abolished, and so we react in
disbelief at our generation's claim of living in a post-
feminist era. Claire doesn't have any contemporaries in her
parish with whom to discuss the paradox of being a
feminist and a Christian. Rachel no longer attends church
and feels more spiritual connection with her writing*

friends anyway. But she, too, wants to dialogue with other young women about feminism and faith. Are only two people enough to form a group?

We remind each other of Jesus' words in the Gospels that whenever two or more are gathered in his name, he will be present, and we set a date in our calendars. On Tuesday evening, over cups of steaming cocoa, we'll begin.

Six

My Red Couch

Sara Irwin

a friend of mine is convinced that God puts things in your path for you to find. Just like when you were a kid, when your mom sometimes put a note in your lunchbox with a piece of candy, my friend Carl believes that God puts cosmic treats in his way all the time. Books sent from God fall on his head out of top shelves, fitting his precise psychological issue of the day. Magazine articles appear miraculously open to just the page he needs. Buddhist writers talk about a similar thing, that the universe gives you the same problems in your life, over and over, until you learn your lesson. As much as I like the idea of a prankster God, having inside jokes with me and helping me to fix my life, I have to say that I am not typically persuaded by this kind of thinking.

But now I am ordained, and "providence" is supposedly one of the tools of my trade. I have become the book pushed out from the top shelf, falling on unsuspecting heads. I'm twenty-five; I have a pierced nose and tattoos. I go to protests against wars and George W. Bush and for GLBTQ[1] equality and a woman's right to choose. I used to shave my head. But becoming an Episcopal priest is the most radical thing I've ever done.

Church has never been easy for me. I didn't spring from the womb "called by our Lord and Savior," or play communion when I was a kid (as some clergy I know did). I served at the altar and did all the other stuff kids in my church did, but once I hit thirteen and started to do my own thinking, I was out of there. Church sounded like otherworldliness and disengagement and prayers to a distant god-man who may or may not grant the requests of the obedient—a celestial butler for those who couldn't afford a terrestrial one. Religious belief looked like a show, something you did because it was expected of you—external performance, not internal identity. This god-man in church was very, very small and very far away. And if I was a girl, and God was a boy, then where did that leave me? Atheism seemed like the obvious answer.

For college, I moved twelve hundred miles away to New College of Florida, where radicals of many stripes were commonplace. We had neither grades nor required courses; we didn't wear shoes to class. And hardly anybody I knew believed in God—and if they did, they certainly didn't talk about it. I dove into gender studies and queer theory. I got interested in religion via philosophy, and eventually took a feminist theology class. And then, finally, there were words for everything that bothered me as a child. God didn't have to be a distant he-man. God was relation and the power of justice making, lovemaking, and truth.

My desire for God formed slowly. Reading feminist theology opened the door for me, but I took a long time to walk through it. As in the Roman Catholic Church, the center of common life in the Episcopal Church is communion. I felt a strange pull toward eucharist, toward the bread and wine that spoke of God's feeding me. Later, there was much to learn: community, the risen Christ among others, love, and fellowship. First, my faith was in my head, critiquing the patriarchal religious tradition and imagining new reality. Then it was in my mouth, receiving the bread of Christ's body—our body—at communion. My heart came last. There was a movement from head to mouth to heart, a way that sacrament and the mystery of participating in this ritual brought me back. It is the bodiliness of eucharist that sustains me, the space between the soul and the lips and the mind, the impossible-to-articulate moment when God is present as we come together. These were outward signs of inward graces that I could not even imagine.

At first, when I started coming back to church, the language used was like a punch in the stomach. I tried not to use the masculine God-language—replacing "he" with "she" here, being silent there—but it still hurt and even now it is hard work. The masculine language that our church uses still forms me and organizes the way I think about God, however I might try to avoid it, however much my liberal parish tries to use inclusive language. Our history is heavy.

There are feminists in the church who do things differently. There are communities where God is not only God the father. But they are few. I simultaneously respect and am frustrated by those for whom separatism is the only option. All the pagans and the "post-Christians" and the goddess worshippers have my admiration and my envy. But part of what I love sometimes is the hard parts, the Nicene Creed and the "Our Father," the parts that I love because they are mine and they are part of me, however they image God. There is a moment in eucharist when the transcendent God is present—when I take God into my own self, in bread and wine that has been prayed over and blessed by my community—that I could not live without. At the same time, it is not lost on me that my own example calls for more female self-sacrifice: asking that we all stay in the burning building so we all can try to rebuild it from the inside. Audre Lorde tells us that we cannot dismantle the master's house with the master's tools. I can only hope that this is not what I advocate.

Church isn't entirely comfortable, but the secular world isn't either. There's always a moment of hesitation when I meet people, a split second of internal *"Please, please, please don't ask me what I do."* It's not that I'm embarrassed about my faith or my church, but I fear the assumptions people will make about me. I think they'll expect me to be boring, or dumb, or ultraconservative. But I'm one of the most leftist people I know, and it's the church that made me that way.

My husband is newly ordained, too, though he looks the part more convincingly than I do. Being a man goes a long way on that score. Finally liberated from student housing when we graduated from seminary last year, it seemed time to make the move from a futon to an actual couch. Having furniture that doesn't fold goes a long way in making a person feel like an adult. So one afternoon, we drove to the Harvard Business School, where Deborah, who was selling her couch, studied and lived. The three of us hit it off, talking about New York City, where we had just moved from and where she was moving to, about small apartments and how the city was still wonderful even if you had to live in a closet. And eventually she asked what we did.

"We're Episcopal clergy," we replied, slurring our words and speaking too quickly.

And she was . . . intrigued. She showed us a case study about a church in Chicago whose advertising practices had been studied by her business class. She wanted to introduce us to her friends who were Roman Catholic. She made us tea, gave us cookies, and talked about being raised a secular-leaning Jew.

And then we got home with the couch, a nice fluffy red one, with wooden feet. We live in a big house in Cambridge, Massachusetts, in the third floor apartment. The stairs are twisty and narrow, but we thought we'd make it. One sweaty and frustrated hour later, I was looking up "Movers" in the yellow pages and dialing the one that advertised "Short Notice."

"I have sort of an emergency," I said into the phone. "My couch is wedged in the stairwell. And I can't get it out."

"I'm by myself," a man said. "Is there somebody there who can help me?"

"My husband and me."

"Alright, I'll be there in half an hour. Might have to pulley it up. That'll cost you."

He sounded sort of resigned, almost disappointed in me that I had done this stupid thing and that he'd be forced to charge me two hundred dollars.

"Whatever. See you soon," I said, thinking that a permanent couch-in-the-stairwell would not make a good impression on the neighbors.

Dave, the moving man, was short, stocky, and about my age. The term "pulley" he had used on the phone made me imagine an enormous piece of machinery that would leave tracks in the lawn I'd have to explain to our landlord, but Dave arrived in a taxicab and carried only a duffle bag. With mild, Zen-like detachment, he assessed the couch situation: "Oh, yeah, that's not getting up that way."

My husband, Noah, helped him to get the couch outside and to the back yard, where Dave intended to bring it up over our balcony and through the back door. I was still vaguely hoping the heavy machinery would appear. Dave attached one strap around the couch and tied a rope to it. I looked up at the distance to my third floor balcony. It was far. It became clear to me at this point that he intended to pull the couch up three floors by hand. I was skeptical.

"Alright," Dave said. "Now Sara, you're going to hold this rope and guide the couch away from the building. Noah, you're going to push up the couch from the bottom, and I'm going to pull, so we can rest it on the second floor balcony."

Suuuure, I thought. Dave looked very strong, but I would feel fortunate if my couch was still in one piece at the end of the day, never mind whether it was in my apartment. It would make a very nice piece of lawn furniture, however overstuffed and impractical in the rain.

Dave bounded up the back stairs to the second floor balcony. If the neighbor was home, she very cleverly ignored us. Dave pulled, and his veins stuck out so far I could see them three floors below. Having done my part, I peered curiously. The red of Dave's face complimented the blue of the painted house trim. The yellow sun and green grass almost made a color wheel.

Dave yelled. I snapped out of it. The couch slipped. "Here it comes down, I can't do it!"

I was thankful that Dave dropped the couch slowly enough for Noah to get out from its path. This scene repeated itself several times until we managed to balance the couch on the wobbly second floor balcony railing. I wasn't certain neighbor Jen would really like to have my couch on her balcony. We rested and regrouped. Noah volunteered to go to the hardware store to buy softer rope and gloves. Dave's hands at this point were crisscrossed with burns, his knuckles bleeding.

Noah was gone for a long, long time. Awkward silence gave way to tentative conversation. We talked about the weather, about Cambridge and the Red Sox. And then the question came.

"So what d'you all do?"

Breath. "We're going to be Episcopal priests, in January. Noah has a job at a parish in the suburbs. I'm going to work in Boston."

An embarrassed shadow crossed Dave's face. "Oh, geez, I hope it didn't bother you that I swore."

"No," I reassured him. "It's fine. I swear, too. You should have heard us coming up the stairs with this thing."

He laughed. I laughed. And that was the part when I started to feel like the book that falls onto the head of the unsuspecting person below. It was clear after a few minutes that Dave had been waiting to have this conversation for some time.

He shared the story of his religious upbringing, how he had been baptized Roman Catholic but his mom became a Jehovah's Witness before he made his first communion, so he hadn't done any of that stuff. And then she had become a Methodist and then she was born again. He had followed her around as a kid, never really knowing what he believed. His dad's family was Greek Orthodox, and he'd been to that church a couple of times, but it wasn't even in English, so he wasn't going to do that again. Dave and I chatted about church, about belief, about politics and how I don't like the president even though he is a Christian. This last comment surprised him.

"Well," the inevitable point came where I had to say it, "the Episcopal Church is great if you're sort of trying to figure things out, because we're very open about things; you don't *have* to believe anything."

"Oh, no, I do, I do. I don't question whether I believe in God," Dave said quickly, caught off guard by this statement and moved to defend his orthodoxy.

"Well, it's okay, I mean, you can question," I replied. "I do. It's important not just to believe what you're told." And then it got a little quiet, maybe a little too intimate. We returned to talking about the weather, and Noah came back with the rope. They tied the rope to the couch, this time in two places so Noah and Dave could pull it up together. It made it up to our balcony and into the apartment (after, of course, taking a few doors off their hinges).

We offered Dave a ride home; it wasn't far. He invited us in for chicken sandwiches. We talked mostly about local bars and music, with a few brushes up against religion mixed in. He showed us the cooking award he got, and he told us about studying nights to get his real estate license and how he smokes a lot because he gets nervous sometimes.

I didn't *feel like* being some kind of girl-wonder-let's-talk-about-spirituality type that day; I just wanted my couch. It would be so much easier, I frequently think, to tell people I'm a graduate student. It's plausible enough; I may in fact be a graduate student again someday if I decide to get a doctorate. Or I could say that I work for a nonprofit, which is true. Not to have to have the conversation, not to have to be associated with the violence that religion has done to so many people. Dave and Deborah were great. But sometimes people avert their eyes, and the conversation ends, the weight of Christianity's past and present intolerance too heavy. Sometimes it's hard closer to home. Sometimes the eye-averters are those who were my own closest friends from before ordination. After years of drift, I am a new and strange person they don't know how to interact with anymore.

You can't be a Christian alone. Even the most secluded, out-in-the-cave hermit is supported by a community that makes solitary life possible. God comes to us through one another, sometimes *as* one another. I might have been an interesting opportunity for Dave to think about his spiritual life, but he and Deborah were books pushed out onto my head, too, reminding me that there is a reason I am still in this church.

None of us can be ourselves alone; as feminists or Christians or Jews or lawyers, we are all ourselves in relation to one another. An analogy from literary criticism comes to mind. The point of deconstruction is that no word has any definition apart from any other word; our own identities work like this, too. All words are defined in relation to other words; all selves are defined in relation to other selves. Truth, then, is inscribed in larger and larger contexts.[2] *We* are inscribed in larger and larger contexts, ultimately in God.

Being a priest is a "twenty-four/seven" identity. It's not a function of having a certain position or role in a community—it's who you are. One of the best descriptions of this comes from Michel Foucault, the French theorist:

> I believe that . . . someone who is a writer is not simply doing his work in his books, but that his major work is, in the end, himself in the process of writing his books. The private life of an individual, his sexual preference, and his work are interrelated, not because his work translates his sexual life, but because *the work includes the whole life as well as the text.*[3]

For Foucault, his life was part of the written text. For a priest, her life is part of the ministering.

It's another version of the old feminist saw, "The personal is political." The political is personal, just as the spiritual is both.

It is exactly *because* religion is so frequently co-opted that I can't just tell people what feels more comfortable for me at that moment. Such a disavowal would not only be untrue, but it would be to reject the God who called *all* of me to be a priest. And it goes both ways; the church, very frequently, would rather that I behave as if I were fifty, not twenty-five. Being ashamed of the female symbol tattooed on my bicep is just as much a threat to my vocation as being ashamed of my ordination. When I tell people I am a student, I'm allowing the radical right to monopolize the religious view. When I stifle my truth as a feminist in church, I'm betraying other feminists. We are never finished being ourselves, never come to the point where everything is neatly reconciled. We can only labor in faith and in hope for God's promises of justice and peace. Sermons are written for the pulpit, but the entirety of your life is your text.

Seven

HAVE SELF, WILL GIVE

Ellie Roscher

I left the Catholic Church in search of another community because I was angry. I was angry when the priest at my grandparents' church would not let me be an altar server at their anniversary mass because I was a girl. I was angry when a female pastor encouraged me to pursue preaching after I was welcomed to preach as a woman in a Lutheran setting, an opportunity unheard of in my own denomination. I was angry that I was supporting a church that valued hierarchy, control, and gender segregation over community, equality, and empowerment of all believers. With a childhood's worth of subtle messages about my (lack of) worth as a woman, I walked away from the Catholic Church with an angry, frustrated, and confused heart. In my twelve years of Catholic education (that did indeed include plaid skirts and pleated jumpers as uniforms), I had been taught that I could come to know God not just through the church, but also in the people and world around me and that truth was not the exclusive property of the Catholic institutional hierarchy. I was convinced that I would find the gospel and a validation of my worth as a woman in a different denominational setting.

I left the Catholic Church because I was skeptical. Skepticism is different from pessimism or cynicism. My skepticism implied that in my doubt lived a faith that may have given up on humans but that would never give up on God. My theology was done in the interrogative, and my lament was my prayer. Deep down, past the muck of human sinfulness in the church, I knew the gospel was about equality. I knew Jesus was a freedom giver and not a controller. I knew that the church should not be about discipline, but about loving our neighbors and ourselves as Christ loves us. I left the Catholic Church in anger and skepticism in hopes of finding a community that preached the gospel of equality and empowered me to encounter the freedom Jesus offers me on the cross. I wanted the community I worshipped with on Sundays to embody freedom, equality, and love of self and others.

Convinced that my Catholic roots and feminism could not simultaneously exist in peace, I went in search of the perfect, nurturing faith community. I went looking for a church where people were so open to the Spirit that space to flourish was created for all people, regardless of their gender, race, or economic status. This search for community led me to celebrate the gospel with Lutheran, Presbyterian, Methodist, and nondenominational Christian communities. One fall morning, when I had just begun my yearlong tenure as a volunteer in the Urban Servant Corps in Denver, this search led me to a Baptist church within walking distance of our volunteers' residence.

Although it was a beautiful and crisp morning, I walked into that church with a heavy heart. I was a plane flight away from my friends and family for the first extended period of time in my life. I was in the depths of the biggest emotional, locational, vocational, and spiritual transition I had faced. With two weeks of working at a homeless shelter under my belt, I was in need of some good news. My first impression was that this church was nothing like the one I had grown up in, which I had attended faithfully each Sunday with my parents and siblings. There were no pews, statues, incense, or holy water. There was no organ, rosaries, or altar. But in this gigantic community, I did not have the time to feel anonymous or out of place. People seemed excited to be at the celebration, and they seemed equally excited that I had come to join them. The drums, horns, and guitars exuded so much energy that there was no choice but to let it be contagious. I surprised myself as I clapped, danced, and really sang for the first time in church. I looked around and smiled, recognizing some of the women experiencing homelessness whom I had met at the shelter. Here was a community that welcomed the outcasts as equals.

And then, suddenly, the tears started. At first, I did not know why I was crying. I was mortified, as I normally only cry in private, but I had no choice. I was connecting with God in an authentic and true way, and the emotions were overwhelming. As the tears turned to sobs, I had a wonderfully raw and honest moment of confession with God. Hurt and gratitude that I had never honored came out of me, and by the end of worship my eyes were tired, but my heart was lighter and filled with the joy only a forgiven sinner can know. It was the first time I can remember really crying at church. A space had been created for me to encounter God as a broken, emotional, and beloved child.

At the end of the celebration, an older man approached me. He was about sixty, with Middle Eastern roots, and wearing a large, wool sweater laced with cologne. With a huge, knowing smile, he said, "God bless you this morning and always," as he gave me an appropriately long and heartfelt hug. He had seen me crying at the beginning of the service. He did not offer me theology or judgment, but comfort and solidarity in a singular embrace and blessing. It was the first time in church that I had been touched and healed by a stranger. Truly, the gospel was alive, and I encountered the God of freedom, equality, and salvation in this space.

One of the truths I encountered that morning in worship was that I would not find a place of peace within a church community until I could find peace within myself. I would not be able to enter the awesome give-and-take relationship with a faith community until I had a strong enough self so that giving of the self and receiving from others did not obliterate my self. Some healing happened that morning that started me on the tenuous road toward being able to hold in tension having a self and giving that self to others.

The path has not been easy. Thinking that I have to be needed to be loved, I tend to work to earn acceptance to the point of losing myself altogether. When I started working at the shelter in Denver, it was easy to be consumed by my job. Because I saw the emergency needs of the homeless women I worked with to be so much more important than my own, I would skip meals and bathroom breaks to help them. I would not take sick days or go on vacation. I never said no. Before long, I forgot that I had needs at all because I was consumed with meeting the needs of others. I would get uncomfortable when people addressed my needs and tried to care for me or love me without me working for it. I literally could not tell another person what I wanted or needed because the needs of my clients had become increasingly more important. I gave of myself to the point that my self began to become invisible, and I no longer gave of that self effectively. I discovered the hard way, through the eradication of myself, the paradox that one must have a self in order to give of the self for others. It became apparent that I could not be a vital part of a community if I did not have a vital self out of which to participate.

❈

To my surprise, despite the many wonderful life-giving aspects I experienced at that Baptist church and at the many other churches I tried on for size, the tension between my feminism and faith did not abate during those years. Celebrating with denominations that ordain women was far from enough to settle my unease with Christian patriarchy. Many of these communities who ordain women continue to use male pronouns for God, pay their male ministers more, and subtly silence the experiences of women. I had begun my naïve quest for the perfect community in hopes of relieving the tension between my feminism and faith, yet I came to realize that no human, Christian community could ever be perfect, and most I had experienced still had a long way to go toward recognizing the full dignity of women.

Although in hindsight I realize I was romanticizing other Christian denominations without acknowledging their human imperfections, I will always cherish my search for the perfect community. I saw some fascinating houses of worship that were homes to beautiful souls who were not afraid to laugh, cry, and sing the gospel into being. I became more open to alternative forms of prayer and worship, and consequently, my romance with God became a bit less academic and a bit more emotionally charged. The tension between knowing God with my heart and with my mind remains in the Spirit's loving embrace and adds vitality to my relationship with God.

Worshipping with multiple communities continually reminded me of how big God is. I had encountered God growing up in the communion and confession of Catholics, but also learned to meet God in the music and the message of the Baptists. Each community is limited, imperfectly seeking to bring God into the lives of its constituents. Yet celebrating God with different denominations challenged me to worship a God who is larger than life, bigger than my imagination, and clearly beyond what any one faith community can express and encapsulate.

Also important for my faith journey, worshipping with other denominations helped me to recognize what Catholics do well and what I missed about my childhood community while also reminding me that Catholics are not the only faith group struggling to empower women as beings created equally in God's image. As my faith and my relationship with God have become more dynamic and less compartmentalized, I have been freer to name both the blessings and the curses of my spiritual inheritance. As a community, Roman Catholics are committed to being aware of and actively fighting for social justice. We understand that being part of a parish means being a light in the community and giving voice to those who are not yet heard. We value education. We are open to encountering God not only in the Bible, but also in tradition, people, nature, and secular sources. And underneath all of these very good reasons to be a Catholic, I ultimately realized that the Catholic Church was my home and that its rhythms of worship and theology are part of my very being. Kathleen Norris expresses the sense of belonging I experience in the Catholic Church:

> I am a practicing Catholic because I believe in the strength of communities of faith and, especially, in the role of ritual as a unifying force that allows people to transcend narrow individualism and reach out to the strangers who mirror our own visage: the moment of the Holy Mass when we turn to our neighbor and offer "Peace be with you."[1]

Another blessing of my spiritual inheritance from the Catholic Church is the veneration of Mary in our tradition. In our study of her, we celebrate the maternal and relational gifts of women that make our community more alive. When I was younger, I was solely comforted that Mary was a woman. Within a male-dominated denomination, hearing priests acknowledge Mary conveyed to me that I could have some worth in the

Catholic Church as a woman. As I matured, I began to love her because she did the will of God. I would imagine myself saying no to a pregnancy that would ruin my sports career and reputation, and I read of Mary to give me courage to decipher God's will even if it called me to do the hard thing or to be in uncomfortable spaces. I moved on to love Mary for being a female who was most likely a robust peasant woman fashioning strength with both muscle and integrity. To be born human, Jesus needed a human mother, so in Mary we celebrate the awesome power of women to be in sustaining communion with a completely dependent human child. The Virgin was not a queen or an aristocrat, but a carpenter's fiancé. In societal terms, she was marginal and marginalized. God's choosing her to bear God's Son yet again demonstrates how the lowly are lifted up and worldly power is humbled.

I do not pray to Mary like I pray to God, but I read about her to ponder her enduringly finite ability to have a strong self while surrendering that self to others. It was only from a place of truly knowing who she was—a beloved daughter of God—that she could agree to bear God's Son. I will forever be awestruck that Jesus, the Son of God, kicked inside her womb. She was a living, breathing woman who lived the Christian tension between having a self and giving that self to others.

As Mary helps me on the personal level, the church helps me on a communal level to create boundaries. "The mother church teaches softly, comforts, and offers protection. In all these ways, she provides a bounded space—a sanctuary—within which her children, now capable of making their own decisions, mature and thrive."[2] The tension between having a self and giving it does not stop at the individual level. Church is a community space that has empowered me to be more fully me through relational love in community.

Recently I moved back to my hometown. I repeatedly heard the name of a Catholic community in the city that was "doing interesting things," and so I decided to take a chance on returning to the denomination in which I was raised. Equipped with my plethora of experiences in other denominations, combined with the anger and skepticism that motivated me to walk away from the Catholic Church in the first place, as well as my renewed appreciation for my Catholic roots, I returned to a Catholic worship context. Even though there were no pews, incense, or altar servers, no stained glass, statues, or holy water, the rhythms of Catholic worship were unmistakable, and I felt at home. I was immediately welcomed into this gigantic, high-energy community. Now again, I was surprised to find myself in an emotional experience of worship, but this time in a Catholic setting. I began to cry, and continued to cry throughout the entire celebration. I cried because I did not think that a Catholic community like this could exist. Here, I was embraced by strangers. Here, I heard a Jewish woman give the homily. Here, I did not feel silenced as a woman. Here, I encountered God as the freedom giver and lover that I had come to know and worship. This Catholic community had created a space where an emotionally charged relationship with God was respected and understood. I felt comfortable coming to worship as a broken and emotional child of God. This Catholic community had created a space where God could remain big despite our sinful and limited nature as creatures. I was reunited with my Catholic heritage in a community that honored and tended to my anger and skepticism. And instead of dominance, discipline, and control, this community believed and lived out the gospel of equality, empowerment, freedom, and relational love.

This community has turned out to be truly Spirit-filled, one that clearly loves God and neighbors with humility and vigor. I strongly believe that worshipping God needs to come to life in loving our male and female neighbors as equals. Church is a real place where this happens. As Kathleen Norris puts it,

It is called salvation, but it begins small, at the local level, in a church that provides a time and space for people to gather to meet a God who has promised to be there. People are encouraged to sing, whether they can or not. And they receive a blessing, just for showing up.[3]

So instead of severing my roots, I choose to find my voice in the conversation. The Spirit has begun to create space of bounded openness for me to explore who I am in Christ and how I choose to articulate that with words and actions in this faith community.

While I have abandoned the search for a perfect faith community, I will not forsake Christianity, because the church has something crucial to offer me as a feminist that secular alternatives for community lack—the gospel of Jesus Christ. The world often tries to tell me who I am. Without words, I am told that I am dirty, dangerous, and sinful because of my menstruation cycle and my gender relation to Eve in the garden. I am too soft, too passionate, too emotional, and too relational. I am the passive receiver. I am the object. I am other. I am defined in relation to man.

But God tells me differently. And Jesus calls the other to himself. Christ, who is beyond gender on the cross, took the shape of a slave and died in the genderless shape of an embrace.[4] He died to offer all of us salvation, love, and mercy. On the cross, Jesus extends to us all that is God's. By naming Jesus Lord, God names us coheirs with Christ. I am God's adored and beloved child. I am offered equality, eternity, and divinity. I am offered the creation of a new heaven and a new earth right now and in the time to come. After the resurrection, we are to see each other with Christ's eyes, as equal brothers and sisters.[5] Christ offers an end to the otherness the world inflicts on women because in our relation to God there is a loss of otherness as we become fully ourselves, letting the God inside of us move and take residence in our hearts and in the world.

Eight

S T R A N G E   B R E W

Kelsey Rice

*D*eep in the coal-laden hills of Tennessee in Appalachia, the tradition of testimony thrives in one Pentecostal church. Even today you may see a wilted old saint, called out by the preacher, rise to her feet and give witness to God's abundant grace in her life. And if you probe deeply into the shadows of memory in that old church, you may see my great-grandfather's young, plow-hardened figure standing up to prophesy in the tongues of the Spirit. When you hear the whispers of the congregation in prayer, you can almost fancy his voice calling out from the grave: "Testify."

Not so long ago, my opportunity to testify came. I was visiting that small country church one Pentecost Sunday and found myself attending Sunday school with a group of relatives. We sat quietly, listening to the teacher explicate on the Pentecost story in Acts 2. Suddenly, a relative sitting next to me said, "Some people interpret this passage to justify the leadership of women in the church. How does it compare to verses in 1 Timothy that call women to keep silent?"

In the silence between that question and the leader's answer, I realized how deep the alienation between the Pentecostal faith of my youth and my current Christian journey had become. I was different from the assorted family surrounding me here, and the difference extended beyond being the "Washington State cousin." Though the well of our faith sprang from the same source, my stream had drifted so far from theirs that, at best, they would call me unorthodox, at worst, condemned.

In the silence, I also knew that I would stay silent; they would remain unaware of the stranger in their midst. I had always been honest with them in saying that I worked with college women for the Presbyterian Church (USA), but I could not bring myself to reveal what that meant: feminist empowerment, GLBT rights, social justice work that criticized the effects of capitalism and American imperialism. I could not testify, except in the most indirect ways, that this had become what the Christian life meant to me. They would never believe that the God speaking to me was the same God to whom they sang their beautiful gospel choruses of praise.

Yes, St. Paul, women still keep silent in the churches.

❖

Why am I what Carol Lakey Hess calls an "underground woman," one of those who, "although they are aware of their feelings and opinions . . . keep them hidden—fearing that their voices will jeopardize their relationships"?[1] Shouldn't my deep conviction of what it means to be feminist and Christian, and my daily work for a Christian feminist organization, lead me to proclaim from the rooftops Jesus' message of liberation to all marginalized people? Yet I am caught in the same trap as many young women from evangelical, conservative backgrounds. We are the feminist women in the middle of the rancorous debates between right-wing Christians and progressive mainline Protestants, not because our beliefs are conservative, but because of the people we know on both sides. Disavowing completely the community of my youth, though it would allow me to come fully into my feminist voice, would be to deny the culture that created me and the wise woman who first breathed life into my fledgling faith. I struggle in tension with that community. Still, love for those there keeps me from confronting it outright.

My parents were the children of southern migrants who settled down near the fruit orchards of Washington State. My grandparents embodied most of the values that form my core today: incredible work ethic, love, thriftiness, and a faith greater than the forces working against them in life. At some point in the distant past, in some faraway, misty Appalachian hollow, they had accepted a faith that freed them from the hardships of their existence. They did not get drunk on the moonshine whiskey that my great-grandfather produced to support his family; they got drunk on the Holy Spirit. When my mother's family came to Washington, they brought their morally rigid Pentecostal beliefs with them and formed a small church. I grew up in that congregation.

My grandmother "drove" Leavenworth Church of God. Some of my earliest childhood memories are of the 1967 blue Chevy Malibu rolling up the driveway and Grandma taking me to Sunday school. As the Sunday school teacher, song leader, and church secretary, she permeated my early faith experiences. She was the "wise woman" who taught me everything I know about the Bible, the Miriam whose strong voice conveyed the love and power of Christ Triumphant. She was also the woman who could not serve on the church board, but who bled herself dry giving everything for her faith community. She has been unshakable in her faith and has never questioned her single-minded devotion to the church.

Despite the powerful female role model I had growing up, I eventually left the Pentecostal Church. At the time, my decision seemingly had no connection to feminism. Simply put, fear drove me away—fear of an angry, authoritarian God who would make me suffer an apocalyptic tribulation, only to judge me unworthy on the Last Day. Today, I see that this fear kept me from questioning my beliefs and critically examining the teachings of the church. My fear of hell rendered me immobile in my spiritual development. Though I had no inkling of feminist theory at sixteen years old, I understand now that a stifling, patriarchal understanding of God almost pushed me out of the church.

I finally found room in the Presbyterian Church to accommodate my faith journey, after years of wandering through a variety of evangelical traditions in search of a home. Leaving the faith completely was never an option for me—the roots ran too deep, and my need for a religious community prevented me from practicing a solitary spirituality. Today, I cannot see the charismatic and evangelical traditions that nurtured my first faith, which supported me in love during the darkest days in my life, as simply evil expressions of patriarchy. I have seen my great-uncle, a Pentecostal minister, tirelessly serve the working-class community in which he lives. I felt the prayers of evangelical college students, who knew nothing more than my name, supplicating God to comfort me in the loss of my father. Countless friends have mirrored God's love to me as we talked about discerning God's call and living a holy life. Despite my theological and social disagreements with evangelicals, there are hues of this tradition that I find incredibly life-giving.

I cannot live comfortably there, however, because I am all too aware of injustices toward women in this society, injustices that many conservative communities bolster through their insistence on the biblical basis for the submission of women to men. I would never have considered myself a feminist until the experience of my father's death. Suddenly, my stay-at-home, traditional mother was a single parent. Despite her high school education being equal to that of my father, it soon became clear that her chances of finding a family-wage job like his were slim. She was forty years old with very little work experience outside child care and no compensating education. Her part-time job working with special needs children ultimately could not support our family. Today my mother tells me how sometimes she looks at the mantle, where my Bachelor of Arts degree sits, and weeps with the knowledge that I will never face the quagmire that she and so many other women her age experience. I wonder how many women like her, accepting the church's teaching that a woman's role is in the home, will find themselves someday abandoned in a system that handicaps them. I cannot look at this system and call it "divinely ordained."

❖

The faith community I have created since then—a diverse hodgepodge of coworkers and friends from high school and college, all women—provides me with a safe space to reconcile the Bible with my own experience. Most of my early understanding of feminism came from academia; I derived my first analysis of gender discrimination from the pages of *Jane Eyre*. The people I have gathered around me in recent years have helped me translate that theory into contemporary terms, seeing injustice as a modern reality rather than a pitiful mistake of our ancestors. More importantly, my connections to other progressive people of faith have challenged me to see the Bible in new ways, ways that are more flexible in responding to the needs of women in the world. Through the examples of the women in my community, I have shifted my understanding of Christian life from following a set of rigid precepts to honoring God with a life of integrated justice.

Moreover, this nurturing community has helped me develop a conviction that in feminist theory lies the heart of the gospel message. Feminism, at its best, challenges the elite patriarchy that privileges some at the expense of the masses. In it lies a message for all, both men and women. Jesus likewise challenged the elite power structure from underneath. A poor carpenter, he condemned those in power while seeking to elevate all those he touched with worth and dignity. I cling to Galatians 3:28, which in my mind sums up both the feminist message and the biblical witness: "There is no longer Jew or Greek, there is no longer slave or free, there is no longer male and female; for all of you are one in Christ Jesus." Christian faith calls us to erase all the socially constructed power dynamics that divide us, claiming our common humanity as children of God.

For me, the tension lies in honoring the traditions that nursed my infant faith, while refusing to compromise my mature beliefs. For deep down, the fear of condemnation still holds some power. In the larger Christian community, many defenders of traditional values perceive feminism as a threat. It is indeed. My beliefs challenge the status quo about relationships between men and women. They also require the church to stop focusing solely on the individual soul and to look outward at the injustices our society unthinkingly perpetuates. Such a church would not look like the faith community of my youth.

I have failed to blend completely the tensions between my more conservative background and my feminist faith, since I can no longer accept uncritically a predetermined, authoritarian interpretation of scripture. In navigating boundaries between the two, however, I strive to define what I value most from each tradition and incorporate it into my life. For instance, my friends often mock me for abstaining from alcohol. Yet I do so not because I believe that indulging in a drink is sinful, but as a way of honoring my faith heritage. In my mother's Pentecostal family, drinking was often characteristic of the poor, working in exploited conditions, whose lives had no hope without faith in God. My family may have been poor in those years, but their moral standards were a viable expression of the hope they had in Christ. I honor that faith through hardship, a faith that I am grateful to acknowledge in my own life. When I refrain from alcohol, it reminds me that I, too, claim Christ's hope, and it sets me apart.

Moreover, I see tinges of the evangelistic spirit in the fervor with which I embrace feminist interpretations of the Bible. My changing scriptural hermeneutics still focus on *sola scriptura* as the heart of the faith. Rather than discarding the Bible completely, as many post-Christian feminists have done, I reinterpret what the Bible says about women and spread the message I discover written there. My favorite aspect of my work in promoting a Christian feminist organization is evangelistic in nature; I reveal the good news of feminist empowerment and liberation through the life and work of Jesus Christ. I have altered the message, but I feel its power with a "Bible-thumper's" enthusiasm.

At the same time, my work with a Christian feminist organization allows me to challenge my evangelical friends and family to consider feminism as a valid Christian expression. I may not directly use the "f" word, but I tell people that I work to empower women to serve God in the church and society. Many of my lifestyle choices—from the fair trade earrings I gave my bewildered grandmother last year for Christmas to my insistence upon developing self-sufficiency by extensive travels alone—are ways I exemplify my emerging feminist consciousness to those close to me. I never tried to force Christianity on others in my youth, and I avoid explicit proclamations of my feminist values now. Yet I hope that even casual observers see the creative blend of Christian feminism in my life.

Finally, I realize that some distinctions can never be fused; different traditions respond to the needs of faith seekers differently. Ultimately, I believe that God honors communities of Christian justice, regardless of their forms. Communities that show their faith by adhering to a particular set of strict moral precepts will never completely resonate for me. Yet they may provide a path for someone who would find the liturgical, intellectual aspects of my faith community stifling. While I hope every faith tradition will eventually work to transform creation from within through a feminist value system, I know that not everyone will come to that place in the same way that I will. Yet those who seek to reach out to others in Christian love and justice serve a purpose in the larger body of Christ.

I find it disturbing that many perceive Christian and feminist factions as mutually exclusive. In reality, the long-term success of feminism in overturning patriarchal systems requires the moral underpinnings of faith communities. As Elizabeth Cady Stanton acknowledged in the 1890 introduction to *The Woman's Bible*, "Let us remember that all reforms are interdependent, and that whatever is done to establish one principle on a solid basis, strengthens all." Christians and feminists fundamentally function on the same moral precept: the world's systems are corrupt and unjust, and we must rise above and work to change them. My faith in Christ gives me the spiritual nourishment for the task. My understanding both of scripture and of feminist theory gives me the roadmap for action.

I live, sometimes comfortably, sometimes not so comfortably, with the identity of a Christian feminist. In embodying that identity, I strive to honor the heart of my Pentecostal faith heritage and the core of my feminist convictions. Sometimes, like in the country church on Pentecost Sunday, I feel isolated in my blend of the two. Yet truthfully, I am not all that different from those around me; I, too, have read the Bible, and it leads me to believe that Christ does not condone gender inequities. I still cling to that evangelistic fervor for scripture, but I apply it to the church in new and challenging ways. Every day, my actions testify to the good news I have found in the gospel.

And when I get discouraged, I remember the words of my own mother, allaying my anxieties about one Appalachian family visit: "You work so that people like me will have more opportunities in the future. I wouldn't be ashamed of that, but proud. And I'm proud of you."

I know then that I have broken through the silence of patriarchy and the silence of fear to reach those I love. And in shattering this silence, I testify to God's irresistible grace that beckons the world with its whispers.

Nine

L I Q U I D W O R D

Christiana Z. Peppard

"¿Cristiana es?" he asks me in a quizzically, emphatically, convinced tone. *"¡Ah, una cristiana!"*

In a shadowy hospital room, the deep stretches of night retreat into linoleum corners. His wife, a resilient Spanish woman with redolent eyes, smiles. *"Soy luterano,"* he proclaims. *"Soy un cristiano."* And pointing to me: *"¡Tu es una cristiana!"*

A name, an identity, an affiliation. *"Soy Christiana,"* I reply, heralding the pun and the truth as one and the same. For my nametag blares *CHRISTIANA* and then, next line, smaller and almost picayune: *Peppard.* To him I am a Christian first, *una cristiana,* a Christian woman. I am struck by the crinkling sound of his hospital sheets and by the soft crevices of age worn onto his bearded cheeks. His liquid morphine drip continues, drop by drop, infusing his veins, relieving the pain of far-progressed cancer.

We wait, immersed in the silence of shared identity, this stranger and I. Perhaps the water of baptism is the fullest, most enduring, most unifying of all substances.

✿

In a thousand innocuous meanderings that we humans tend to forget to notice, water permeates our lives. It hovers on the tips of waxy leaves, or dribbles down the drain, or hums in unending ocean currents, or seeps stealthily into fertile soils. I am from arid country, raised on the plains of Colorado, where water is scarce and sweat shrinks from the sweltering sun well before it can congeal into droplets. During droughts in that region, even the reservoirs desiccate. They become dry, cracked shells, enormous abandoned carapaces. The swimming pools where I swam competitively were the only places where you could be cloaked with water indefinitely.

I now live in Connecticut. Here, at the interstices of divinity school and humid climate, my understanding of water has changed. In the height of summer the driest place is, ironically, the shore, for the breeze whisks away water droplets and incorporates them into the precipitation cycle above the ocean surface. Inland, we do not have that grace, and beads of sweat are permanent companions unless wiped away.

Water, like oxygen, is one thing without which bodies cannot live. Without this most fundamental physiological substance and sustenance, we would not only fail to flourish; we would cease to exist. Beyond our bodies, water flows freely into the infinite variety of our physical surroundings. Water does not discriminate; it simply cascades (or trickles), and nourishes, and sustains. Water cleanses and restores. This most primary and abundant of earthly substances, this most life granting of liquids, is an apt metaphor for grace. Like the water that feeds our bodies, grace sustains our souls. Grace does not discriminate; it finds its way into every corner of human life, regardless of gender, race, sexual orientation, economic status, or level of education. Both water and grace remind us of our contingency, of our very human composition and very human need. And the water of baptism—literally the water of grace—is a reality that cannot be washed away.

❖

In the name of the Father, the Son, the Holy Spirit, in the name of all that is holy. The words flow over you, the water claims you, and you are changed. Water, words, and witness are all that is required for baptism to stick. Three little elements, so constitutive of our lives; yet so ephemeral! The pastor wipes away residual droplets with a towel. The words dissipate into the still air of the sanctuary, and the community of witnesses heads home after another Sunday service. How fleeting it all seems!

Yet the water of baptism spiritually marks a human body that will celebrate, suffer, and change throughout life. In baptism, God "officially" encircles and indwells the lives of human beings. We learn (and remember) that God will journey with us through the dynamism of our existence, into illness and ultimately into death. The water of baptism does not evaporate; neither does our identity. We are God's own, yes; but we are also members of a community writ large.

My baptism was particularly off the beaten path. Preparing for marriage to my Catholic husband required the proper certification (apparently my name, which the *luterano* in the hospital had so accurately noted, did not reveal my authenticity before God in the eyes of the Roman Catholic Church). Certification of baptism seemed to be merely a minor logistical hurdle. I was unconcerned. Thus, uncertain of the details, but certain that my grandmother had in passing affirmed that I was baptized, I called her and learned that I was baptized not in a church—"Oh heavens no, darling! No church, no priest!"—but in a kitchen sink.

Yet for a brief moment, I heard only the words "no church, no priest." I was under the impression that I had never been baptized at all. The bottom seemed to drop out of my world. I was standing on a florid green carpet in the middle of my rented apartment, ten months after graduating with a degree in human biology from one of the country's most secular universities, living in a house with two divinity students and a molecular biologist. The contours of the room blurred together, and I stumbled back toward a chair. After vehemently eschewing Christianity for a decade, I had come face to face with the fact that my identity was definitively linked to the waters of baptism—and to the idea of belonging to a Christian community.

As it turns out, when I was one month of age and roughly the size of the Thanksgiving turkey she was preparing, my Catholic grandmother—concerned for the fortitude and flourishing of my soul—surreptitiously baptized me in the kitchen sink. My parents, a Christian Scientist and an estranged Catholic, were not in favor of baptism and were thus unaware of the clandestine way in which my grandmother and the Holy Spirit had claimed my soul for God.

In retrospect, I think it was an utterly appropriate entrance into sacramental life, in the most quotidian of settings, and amidst the clamor of familial Thanksgiving preparations. Droplets of grace anointed me before cascading into the kitchen sink and, from there, into the labyrinthine pipes of central California. Grace, like water, does not necessarily prefer marble fonts or reverent silences.

❀

Prompted by this story, I began to wade into my history of faith. Growing up as a Christian Scientist, I had perceived God as a distant, diffuse, nonliturgical presence, one that I tried to tap into through the language of prayer. "Father Mother God, loving me," was the beginning of the Christian Science prayer that I intoned nightly. "Guard me when I sleep; guide my little feet up to thee." *Father Mother God.* Only when I came to divinity school, only when I started attending Catholic mass with my husband and was overcome by the liturgy, only when I became brave enough to encounter all the iterations of Christianity that I had eschewed for a decade, did I realize the profound simplicity of that Christian Science prayer. Father Mother God. The spoken word is powerful, is evocative, is slippery.

As a child, however, scripture—the written Word—was significantly more recalcitrant. In fact, it was flatly two-dimensional. In my most vivid Sunday school memory, I received a jumble of words, each on an individual scrap of paper, and was instructed to compile them into some biblical passage—Psalm 23? David and Goliath? I was sheepish because I didn't know the passage by heart. I was more aware of the details than the goal, which I found incomparably dull. Not only did the Scotch tape fail to stick in any satisfactory way (ending up irritatingly entwined around my cuticles), but also the words were so *flat* afterwards. I remember puzzling over the way that each scrap of paper quivered right before I plunked it onto the page. But, alas, there was no movement after the plunk.

Constrained to two dimensions, the words were orderly but lifeless. They did not fit well together and sat there in perpetual torpor. These ancient words of some ancient person's faith had no claim on me. They were strangers, occasionally hostile. And so once my family stopped attending the Christian Science church, I felt no compulsion to follow scripture or Jesus or attend official worship. That inclination was exacerbated by a scarring experience at a friend's church camp when I was thirteen. During a Bible study on Revelation, I protested that surely a God of love would not condemn people in the Eastern Hemisphere, or the Jews for that matter, because they hadn't accepted Jesus Christ as their personal Lord and Savior. Since the historical-critical school had not yet come to town, my protestations were not charitably received: I was told that unless I recanted this line of thought and professed my belief in Jesus Christ, I, too, was going to burn for eternity.

God, I decided, definitely did *not* reside in scripture, and the Trinity could take the first bus out of town, thank you very much.

Looking back, I am surprised at how many of my feminist convictions are embodied in those two stories. Acknowledging that God is father and mother. The thirteen-year-old girl shocked at the possibility of injustice to a million unknown faces a world away. The conviction that God could not, did not, categorically condemn God's own people. The distress of an adolescent who was told by camp counselors and close friends that conformity was the only way to assure oneself of salvation. Despair. Anger. Disbelief. Fast-forward thirteen years: I am clambering onto a fuller shore of faith. But, to put it mildly, it has been a very long swim.

❖

Perhaps my two primary feminist longings are not surprising, given my context. First: I deeply desire fairness. Second, entailed in the first: I desperately seek a world in which we recognize the particularity, complexity, uncertainty, and vulnerability inherent in each human life. For it is only in this type of mutual recognition that we can understand each other—and only then can we act justly. Of course I do not mean to say that there are no common themes in human experience. I simply insist that the pitch and refrain and tone and crescendo and rhythm of those themes are remarkably contingent. In other words, homogeneity is not a dominating feature of our world.

To my surprise, I found support for this feminist vision in a passage of scripture. "As many of you as were baptized into Christ have clothed yourselves with Christ," Paul writes in the "baptismal formula" of Galatians 3:27–28. "There is no longer Jew or Greek, there is no longer slave or free, there is no longer male and female. For all of you are one in Christ Jesus". Of course, I am not the first to revel in these words. Philosophers and exegetes have spent much time with this passage. But it is not the history of interpretation that intrigues me. Instead, I am drawn in by the poetry, the astonishing boldness, of this little claim.

Quite simply, I believe that to be clothed with Christ in baptism is *not* to replace one's identity with the cloak of an amorphous, unindividuated humanoid. Yes, Christ's identity is unifying and it does, importantly, encompass our own. But that does not mean that our identities are inconsequential or that they can be discarded or denied. Indeed, to radically deny our bodily or experiential selves is patently impossible. Like the Galilean throngs in need of Jesus' healing, we are afflicted by life situations diverse and plentiful, whether we like it or not, and whether we choose it or not. Human needs and human realities are as particular as the infinite strands of DNA from which human bodies come.

Isn't it, therefore, plausible that our "oneness" in Christ is formed and found *because of* all of our personal journeys, self-descriptions, economic distinctions, sexual orientations, professional choices, and chromosomal concatenations? Isn't it possible that in our individuality we are *called* to look beyond ourselves, called by the trickling of water and grace that unite us in our particularities? Such a call—to fairness, to mutual recognition, to justice—is, like water, omnipresent. It is a call that relishes the diversity of life and that can only be lived out in a community that celebrates the particularity of its members. It pervades all languages, images, experiences. *This* is the fundamental source from which and to which all things particular flow.

Further, Paul hints at something even more profound: Baptism *does not work* without diversity. If humans were homogenous, it would be rather redundant for Paul—and for all baptismal liturgies over the past two millennia—to remind us that we have so much in common. Baptism only has meaning when the infinite expressions of human life persist. Expression of self comes naturally to us; as heirs to the Western philosophical tradition, we put much stake in our individual identities. Baptism simply asks us to remember that in our differences we can recognize each other and join in fellowship together. To be one in Christ requires the presence of *both* Jew and Greek even as it negates those racial identities. It requires slave and free even as it speaks to a desire for justice. It recognizes physiological differences even as it points to the intrinsic worth of all persons, no matter what their sex or gender. If we cease to recognize the myriad ways of being human in this world, if we insist on simplistic homogeneity, if we fear those who are different or if we disdain those who disagree, our ability to be one in Christ fails.

In fact, Galatians 3:27–28 prompts me to think that all of our humanly devised categories fall short, for we see only fragments of life's fullness. We can never fully get a grip on the world. Why? Because, on the one hand, we are not God; we are finite. And, on the other hand, because the world—and life in it—is always changing. To focus on the human element, our bodies are dynamos of change. Our bodies and our identities fluctuate with every experience we have in the world (sexual, religious, gustatory, or otherwise). We observe, absorb, and integrate nuances of the world around us; we evaluate and choose; we act. Stasis is not a possibility of human life, and no two lives are identical. Hence the variety of changing bodies and identities in our world tells me that "being one in Christ" implies a vastness of which our human minds can barely conceive. And this is only a sliver of the presence of God, one drop in an undulating current.

✻

For all are one in Christ Jesus. It certainly sounds nice. But is it truly possible to believe in the communality that this language promises? After all, our world is rife with hate, rape, genocide, war, and conflict; it is replete with the failures of humans to treat other persons as beings deserving of love and respect. In such a world, it seems rather inane to say that we are all one in Christ Jesus. It seems idealistic to say that community is as broad as Jew and Greek, as Christian Scientist and Roman Catholic, as eastern and western, as all the bodies swimming in the baptismal waters of this world.

And yet the waters of baptism do not discriminate. Further, the substance of baptism, the liquid Word, is *everywhere.* Where water is concerned, the line between sacrament and sacrament*al* becomes very tenuous indeed. Water and grace seep into the most intractable and inaccessible places and persons. Who is to say that this diffusion is not its own grace? Who are we to say, from God's view, who counts and who does not?

"¿Cristiana es?" the dying man in the hospital bed, whom I have never before met, asks. *"Soy luterano,"* he adds. To which I can only respond, *"Soy cristiana."* With so little in common, we share much, for the little that we do share is precious indeed. The noun "Christ," the noun-or-adjective "Christian," an identity, a name: at root God claims, changes, and demands an account. We are interminably accosted by the contingency of our bodies, by the suffering and iniquity that characterize much of life. Yet the words and water and witness of baptism exclaim our oneness. They suggest that perhaps we can, in all our diversity, recognize and honor each other. They hint at the possibility that we might even exist together in communities of justice.

And so I cannot help but know that water is salvific, whether of kitchen-sink baptism or rivers or rain. It is both sacramentally and biologically essential. Its cascading meanings clamor for us to drink deeply, to be healed and replenished, and to seek life's variegated fullness. I suspect that such a proclivity toward water is, at root, a tendency toward grace. To let ourselves be buoyed up by grace—which, like water, does not discriminate—is perhaps the greatest plunge of all.

Ten

A Walking Contradiction

Monique Simpson

"Some preachers have a problem with women preaching, but I
don't as long as it's under a male's authority."

As the last words left his lips, his Santa-like body spun toward the congregation. Rapidly raising his index finger, he expressed the stern look of a father who was setting the rules for
rowdy teenagers. As pastor, he was the ultimate authority of this
black Baptist church in Arlington, Texas.

His harsh statement sailed smoothly through the sea of
Christian ears like Bible verses and favorite hymns. But, in my
ears the words exploded like bombs, startling my soul and awak-
ing my consciousness. If I were in a cartoon, smoke would have
steamed from my flushed face. Instinctively, I tried to calm myself
by denying what I had heard.

"Did he say what I thought he said?" I incredulously asked
my female friend who sat next to me.

She nodded and shrugged her shoulders in a "No big deal; I've heard it before" manner. But I had not heard it before. We weren't in Houston, but I was definitely experiencing a problem in Texas.

It was Mother's Day 2002. I was sitting in the back of one of those megachurches for which Texas is famous. In a single building (sometimes as large as a sports arena), hundreds of people wearing their "Sunday best" (their most fashionable, but respectable clothing) filled pews (well, actually at that church it was individual chairs) to share fellowship with people you wouldn't recognize if you passed them in the grocery store. The preacher was about as personal as a singer performing in a stadium.

Despite the impersonal nature of the place, each Sunday attendees jumped to their feet, walked down the aisle with excitement, and joined the church. And I had been one of them. Although I would only be in the Dallas/Fort Worth area for four months as a *Star-Telegram* newspaper intern, I had promised myself that I would return home to Los Angeles a baptized believer. It wasn't that I needed the water to save my soul, because I had already accepted Christ into my life years earlier. It was that I knew the ritual of baptism created a special bond between Christians. Brothers and sisters in Christ held each other accountable for living by faith and gave encouragement when doubt flooded the soul. Also, being baptized in a black church served as an easy entrance into the black community, something I had been longing for since high school. Some African Americans viewed me as a "white girl" because I wasn't raised in the inner-city and didn't spice up my speech with slang. In a large church, I figured I would be able to connect with African Americans who had similar backgrounds, thus allowing me to feel connected to my ethnic community.

On top of all my reasoning about the importance of joining a black community of brothers and sisters in Christ, the biggest reason I joined that church in Texas was that I had stopped growing with the Lord. My journey with God had begun during a Bible study at UCLA's minority summer program; I had raised my hand when the student leader asked if anyone wanted God to make his or her life better. In the leader's dimly lit dorm room, I sat on a twin-size bed with five other freshmen and asked God to be a part of my life. God accepted my invitation, but as months passed, my walk with God became superficial. Faith lost its top priority slot in my life; school, career, and love desires dethroned it. I was left spiritually empty. With a self-imposed deadline, I decided to fill that void by joining a community of faith to help strengthen my walk with God. But in rebuilding my relationship with God through a faith community, I needed to address the issue of sexism in the church.

❖

Since that summer evening in '97 when I first opened my heart to God and confessed Christ as my savior, I constantly debated how much of Christianity I would incorporate into my life. I didn't fully agree with limiting women's roles in the church, and I was pro-choice. Some more traditional Christians said my reluctance to accept conventional church teaching was my spirit battling my flesh. But it was, and is, more than that. I was struggling to maintain independent thinking in the Christian and secular realms of the world and in the black church where the two realms meet for me.

It would be too easy to let a male preacher dictate my standards of living. Similarly, I don't want *Ms. Magazine* shaping my complete understanding of womanhood. Balancing Christianity and feminism is the only way for me to create my identity. It is a struggle; however, most days I am successful because I admit that I'm a walking contradiction.

While in college I managed my balancing act by not firmly planting myself in God's Word. I regularly attended church and Bible study, but I selectively applied the messages to my life. As my graduation date approached and big life questions began swirling in my head like a crazed housefly, a spiritual alarm buzzed within me: *Improve your relationship with God.*

For about a year, I ignored the ringing. Committing to God was a permanent decision. But the day arrived when my soul aligned with my mind, and I knew it was time. I joined that church in Texas and the family of Christ.

Yet as I sat in that same church on Mother's Day 2002 and heard the pastor explain that women could preach as long as it was under a man's authority, every antireligious, feminist thought rushed through my head, making me doubt my decision.

As if the preacher's comment wasn't enough to turn me away from Christianity, the morning sermon, delivered by the preacher's wife, surely should have. Expecting praise for the enduring work of mothers, I was shocked to hear the church's first lady deliver one of the most antifemale speeches I had ever heard, depicting women as nothing more than deceiving Jezebels. Perhaps she had mixed up her dates because not one uplifting or affirming comment about women was made.

I left that Baptist church after the service and never returned. I was deeply disturbed by this type of "conservative Christianity," as my friend next to me in the church had referred to it. How could I, a woman who came of age in the '90s, who grew up in Los Angeles, who had completed a college degree and learned to think for herself, ever find a spiritual home in a brand of Christianity that taught women to let men do all of the thinking? I longed for a place that would continue to foster my relationship with God, but I was not sure I was willing to sacrifice my feminist beliefs in order to be part of such a community.

❖

That night beneath the green glow of ceiling stars, I lay in bed questioning if I really wanted to be associated with this female unfriendly religion. I had always felt a little uncomfortable calling myself a Christian because people throughout history have used this title to justify committing hideous crimes. However, I did not, and do not, doubt that Christ died for my sins. His sacrificial blood will save my soul on judgment day. Since I believe faith is crucial for salvation, I knew I had to work toward some sort of compromise. I could not leave Christianity, but I also wanted to be able to affirm my feminist beliefs.

Then I thought about not attending church. As a friend regularly told me, "Why do I need to go to church? God is always with me." (Of course, she liked to say this as we drove to Deep Elm for a night of dancing in Dallas, and I told her we had to leave early because I had to go to church the next morning.) But why was my soul continuously searching for a church community if this community wasn't necessary to know God?

The answer was simple. No individual is as strong as a group. A single feminist is just a wave crashing onto the sidewalk of sexist institutions. Yet a group of organized feminists is a tidal wave, crushing windows, forcing more Americans to take notice of societal problems. Individual women and African Americans who worked together won my civil rights. I would only be able to strengthen my relationship with God through involvement with others who are on the same spiritual path.

With the support of my brothers and sisters in Christ, I cannot fall victim to the world's pain. When I do not attend church regularly, I feel society's negativity seeping into my soul, making me bitter, angry, and frustrated. I mentally withdraw from my surroundings and go into my "whatever" phase. I say "whatever" to problems that do not directly affect me. I become indifferent to everyone and everything from the homeless man breathing on me to upcoming elections. I just search for happiness and try to escape the world's misery. But true feminists and Christians, like civil rights activists, know that "whatever" is a sign of a coward with little faith. How could I let go of either my feminism or my

Christian faith? Plus, how could I contemplate turning my back on the black church, a place where I could find community with those who share my ethnicity?

✿

Originally created because whites did not wish to worship with freed slaves, the black church has become the cornerstone of our community. It is like a cultural center where ethnic minorities remember their culture's uniqueness in the face of the homogenizing forces of American society.

Whether I sing hymns with Baptists, clap my hands with Pentecostals, tap my foot with African Methodist Episcopalians (AME), or shout "Amen" with members of other dominations, I worship with African Americans to be empowered. Sitting shoulder to shoulder with people who are dealing with the same brown-skin prejudices is comforting. Friends of other ethnicities sometimes deny that race is still a prevalent issue in the United States. But in the black church, no one doubts the realness of race. Church leaders historically have spoken out against mistreatment of minorities. Many of the civil rights movement's key leaders came from the pulpit, such as Rev. Martin Luther King Jr. Worshipping with African Americans helps me to integrate my ethnic heritage into my identity, alongside my feminism and Christianity.

However, there has always been a conflict afflicting African American women: are women's rights as important as combating slavery's legacy? I have heard the argument that women's rights cannot be seriously sought until racial equality is established. But at the current rate of progress, generations of African American women will be born and buried before our issues are addressed. We can no longer quietly cook dinners in the church kitchen nor can we sit passively in the church as I did that Mother's Day in

Texas. Change won't come from the weak and timid, but from women who possess a strong sense of self and faith.

❊

Upon returning home to Los Angeles, I began attending church with my family. It was a black Baptist church in the San Fernando Valley. It had a few hundred members, and the pastor was somewhat progressive. A former soldier who was in his second marriage, he appeared to be opened-minded about women's role in the church. In honor of women's history month, women preached the morning sermon during March. The women, unlike the female speaker in Texas, encouraged and motivated women to be strong in their faith and in life. And not once did the pastor state that these women were preaching under a male's authority.

I enjoyed seeing women confidently deliver a biblical message from a female perspective. It was a sign that the black church was moving into the new millennium. However, the church sometimes stumbled backwards. Some Sundays I wondered if any progress had been made at all.

My pastor would tell young ladies "to keep your panties up and your skirts down." But he always forgot to tell young men to keep their "friend" down and their zippers up. He placed the burden of "purity" in women's laps and didn't point out men's responsibilities. I sighed loudly as he spoke his old-fashioned clichés. My older brother and younger sister, who sat next to me, snickered. They knew my views and found it funny whenever I became upset.

I was disappointed by the pastor's comment, but my desire to personally know God was the real reason I awoke early Sunday morning when my bed's warmth tempted me not to leave it. I couldn't let a man stand between eternal salvation and me. Although the patriarchy of the church rankled, I knew I could not grow in faith on my own. In July 2002, I joined the church and was baptized the first Sunday in August.

Two years later I found the courage to question traditional teaching about women's roles. I realized sighing wasn't speaking out; it was noisily doing nothing. My church leaders needed to know my thoughts.

During a discussion on obedience in my Sunday school class, my teacher, a deacon, brought up marriage and submissiveness. As a married, middle-aged man, he had no problem with wives being submissive to their husbands. He favored a traditional, woman-as-homemaker, man-as-breadwinner type of family. He assumed that once married, women would change their last names, do most of the household chores, and happily obey their husbands' decisions.

"That's crazy!" I exclaimed. "I didn't go to college to be submissive to any man. I will maintain some independence and have an equal say in decision making," I told him and the rest of our class.

"Sounds like you're trying to be a man," he said calmly.

"I'm not trying to be a man," I said in a vivacious voice. I sighed and paused long enough for my voice to return to normal. "My independence shouldn't threaten your manhood," I told him, looking directly into his eyes. He said it didn't.

After our discussion, we assembled in the church sanctuary with the other Sunday school classes. Standing in front of the room, my teacher posed the question that I had asked him. "If a young lady goes to college and starts her own career, why should she be submissive to her husband?"

Laughter instantly filled the room. My pastor lowered his head as he chuckled. Older women turned to each other smiling. The lawyer in front of me joked, "That's what the Bible says," implying that his wife, who is also a lawyer, didn't play the submissive role. But the female pianist answered in a matter-of-fact way, loud enough for everyone to hear, "Because the Bible says so."

As the laughing faded, I sat in the pew, embarrassed and upset. I hadn't expected my teacher to share our conversation with the entire congregation. Yet thinking back on it, I noticed that I was making progress in giving voice to my beliefs; instead of walking out of the church, as I did in Texas, I raised an important question in the midst of the community. I knew that my thinking was different than most of my fellow churchgoers, but I had come to a place of confidence where I was no longer willing to sacrifice my feminist beliefs on the altar of silence. I will never be persuaded that women should be submissive to their husbands, and I hope to continue voicing my dissent toward my church's understanding of women's roles.

Some may wonder why I have not switched churches, but I do not believe church shopping would help. While my current church is conservative in how it construes relationships between men and women, it is much more progressive on other issues than many black churches I have encountered. Further, I often wonder if the role I am called to play in this community is to challenge it to change its conservative views about women. Maybe through my relationships with community members, people will be persuaded, however slowly, to align their Christianity with some feminist beliefs. Recently, as our church prepared for "men's month," I made a point to speak with that same deacon who had shared my question in front of the entire congregation. I told him that sexist language was not appropriate and that I would be listening to make sure it did not creep into his sermon. Change has to begin somewhere, and urging this deacon to be aware of his use of language is at least a good place to start.

So I stay. I stay because salvation is important, because I want to grow in faith, and because I just might be able to influence some change for the better.

❖

Nothing in this world, including Christianity and feminism, is perfect. I accept the aspects of the Bible that testify to God's love for us and continue to question church tradition that favors male leadership and preaching. I have feminist beliefs but I also believe women should be held responsible for their behavior and not rely on the "victim" role. I long for women to be confident, to be more comfortable with themselves, so that they can have the strength to voice their opinions and to stand independently.

With each sunrise, I try to balance my Christian, feminist, and African American identities, for all are important parts of my sometimes contradictory identity. My Christian identity calls me to contribute to the greater good of society and to act with compassion toward those around me. Being a feminist allows me to speak out against gender inequality and has helped me name my self-worth as a woman. My African American roots provide me with an understanding of my heritage and a passion for social justice. Many weeks it is overwhelming. The world swirls too fast, and I become dizzy from trying to distinguish myself among others' blurry images of womanhood. I feel the expectations and obligations of each of my identity groups suffocating me. *African Americans think this . . . Christians oppose this . . . Feminists believe this. . . .* The demands of loyalty never end.

Rapper Mos Def once said, "Sometimes I don't wanna be a soldier; sometimes I just wanna be a man."[1] I, too, just want to be a woman. But it is difficult creating an identity amidst conflicting ideas of what it means to be a person of darker complexion with a vagina who calls herself a Christian. Yet I begin to fuse the contradictions of living into the strength of love of self through a deep understanding of my relationship with God, which is fostered by my community of brothers and sisters in Christ.

Eleven

Why Do I Stay?
Finding Strength in the
Community of Believers

Mary Louise Bozza

a few hours after I was born, I was shaken awake by a
feisty, retired Maryknoll nun, Sister Amata. "Let me
see her eyes," she insisted, to the dismay of my demure
and gentle Italian grandmother, who had most likely
just finished lulling me to sleep. Sleep could wait. Sister Amata
had been anxiously awaiting my birth for months. She was a good
friend of my parents, and I imagine that she, along with many
others, felt great excitement that two such loving and energetic
human beings were bringing new life into the world. I also imagine that she was even more excited to become a surrogate second
grandmother to this new child. My newborn eyes opened to a
kindred spirit staring intensely into my soul.

As a little girl, I spent countless hours in the kitchen of the convent in which Sister Amata and her compatriots lived, where I could find my own hand-sewn gingham apron hanging in my very own cubby hole, ready for whatever adventures Sister Amata felt like cooking up for us on that given day. I learned to weave placemats from strips of brightly colored construction paper and to make deliciously lumpy applesauce from fresh fall apples harvested from the trees speckling our backyard. Sister Amata nurtured in me creativity and a strong sense of self. She abounded in generosity, honesty, and enthusiasm and subtly convinced me that I was capable of doing anything that my little heart desired. While we labored over our masterpieces of construction paper and clay, she indulged me with brilliant stories of her adventures around the world as a missionary.

Sunday mornings, unlike most children my age, I anxiously awaited our trip to church. Sister Amata would be waiting for us at the door, ready to grab my little hand and proudly march me through the tomb-like gathering of pious older women, straight up the center aisle to sit with her in the very front pew so that we could be "closer to Jesus." Sometimes the giggling, and often irreverent, pair of us managed to make a bit of a scene and inspire snickers and scoffing from the church "regulars." But none of that mattered a bit to my special friend. She loved Jesus and his church with a fierce passion—a passion that had been strong enough to coax her away from the material pleasures awaiting her as a young, effervescent girl half a century earlier; a passion that helped her confront countless authorities, even at gunpoint during World War II; a passion that sustained in her an overflowing joy, even as she battled cancer during the last years of her life. While she was in the hospital, her love of Christ remained unbreakable and inspirational to every friend who visited and every nurse and doctor she encountered. She never stopped being the one to assure us— even the doctors—that everything would turn out as it should because she trusted that Jesus was taking care of her. And he was.

Years after Sister Amata passed away, when I was a little older, my mother shared with me some newspaper articles and testimonials written about her. The articles, telling of her extraordinary strength and courage in the face of physical and spiritual attack from wartime authorities, and beautiful testimonials by children and friends whom she had taught or catechized, were poignant reminders of the stories with which she had entertained me as a young girl. Tears came to my eyes as I sat at our kitchen table and realized the great gift of friendship and love she had given to my family and me.

As she merrily bounced around the church in her plain black smock, sometimes wrapped in her beloved scarlet cape, Sister Amata was teaching me to love Jesus and his church as *she* had come to know them by loving and respecting everyone she met and by fighting for what she believed. She firmly believed that spunky little me, though sometimes overly chatty and bossy, was welcome in that stuffy, quiet church just as much as the white-haired women counting the beads of their rosaries, wearing frowns and shushing us as we joyfully took our front-row seats to be with Jesus each Sunday.

❖

Two decades later, I am still discovering the hopes and dreams Sister Amata nourished in my active, young soul so many years ago. Only now am I beginning to realize how much I was influenced by her powerful example of truly being on fire with the love of Christ and of then being compelled to invest that love in other people.

Along with a great appreciation for colors and noise and lumpy applesauce, Sister Amata instilled in me self-confidence, the courage to be original (and sometimes even controversial), and a hearty passion for life. She also taught me that it was important to respect the ways in which the Holy Spirit was working for change in the church while taking the time to admire, and even bask in the beauty of, our Roman Catholic tradition.

Over the years, I have encountered many people who do not agree with Sister Amata's inclusive understanding of "the church" as a community of holy people who believe in Jesus Christ, not just those of particular denominations. Many Roman Catholics who *do* agree with such inclusive ideas consequently have found it restrictive or even impossible to remain part of an organization that sometimes does not validate such claims. The question then becomes: why do I still choose to associate myself with this community? A community that restricts its decision-making powers exclusively to celibate men. A community that proclaims that women, frankly, are not meant to do certain things. A community that refuses to acknowledge or even listen to many of my opinions, specifically those related to my femininity. A community that doesn't seem to embrace many of the things that Sister Amata taught me to cherish so dearly.

Why do I stay?

There is a simple answer: Sister Amata showed me that the church could never be bound by rules or definitions, no matter how hard anyone tried. The church she revealed to me was a beautifully mismatched, hodge-podge, imperfect, and human community of believers, just as accurately embodied by St. Francis of Assisi, my grandmother, Mother Teresa of Calcutta, or even myself, as it is by the infamous succession of popes and bishops. And so if I take the time to explore and listen carefully to the world around me, amidst the dark stories of the abuses of power and judgmental and exclusive attitudes, I am able to find unending beauty in the communion of holy people that is the sacramental church. The church is manifested in all kinds of people, through all types of prayer, through irrational love, and through the gifts of the sacraments. But the search for these threads of light and grace is not always as easy as it may seem.

❖

My brother and I inherited an American-immigrant breed of Catholicism, certainly based upon the pillars of prayer, justice, love, and charity, but with hefty measures of guilt and obedience thrown in. My parents were both Catholic-school educated all of their lives, and traces of the pre-Vatican II ideals that they had been taught in school sometimes reared their heads.

Even though my parents and my youth group leaders urged me to question my faith and nurture it as something personal and unique, a lot of what guided my early faith life was a sense of obedience: living according to the teachings of the Catholic Church was the right thing to do. For me, taking ownership of my own faith was a gradual and difficult process. It was certainly made easier by remembering what Sister Amata had taught me, by critically examining my experience of relationship with Jesus and his church, and also by getting to know the greater community of Catholics extending through centuries and all sorts of cultures.

I learned about the lives of the saints who modeled traditionally feminine virtues—St. Bernadette, St. Therésè of Lisieux (the little flower), and the Blessed Mother—from my gentle, devout grandmother and my uncle, Father Nick. Eventually I stumbled upon the feisty women saints, too, those whom I'm sure Sister Amata would have introduced me to, had she lived longer. These women became my role models and spiritual companions through the pages of their journals and the stories written about them.

While studying abroad in Spain, I began to read about St. Teresa of Ávila. She radically reformed the Carmelite Order in the face of great opposition, stood up to the Inquisition, was a great mystic, and was named the first woman doctor of the church. While studying ethics in Rome, I encountered St. Catherine of Siena, another doctor of the church, and a laywoman, who bravely urged the pope to have the courage to reform the church and the papacy. While living at a Catholic Worker community one summer, I fell so in love with the writings of Dorothy Day and her commitment to living out the radical Christian gospel that I chose to write my senior thesis in college about her theology. All of these women exemplify inspirational spiritual courage and strength in the face of great opposition, and each in her own way was able to help the church to reform and grow.

As I grew older, I also began to see my own mother anew as a Catholic woman. I had always taken for granted that she was involved in the life of our parish, heading the religious education program and teaching confirmation classes. Perhaps more importantly, though, beyond her work in the parish, I admire her for the ways in which she allows her religious beliefs to influence her politics and all of her decisions and actions. She is boundlessly selfless and loving, and yet she still manages to be very much a feminist. She is both faithful to and critical of the church. Most importantly, her experience of church is rooted in a personal relationship with Jesus.

Sister Amata, my parents, my youth group leaders, and the examples of St. Teresa, St. Catherine, and Dorothy Day convinced me of my own authority as a Catholic as I saw how they had claimed the church as their own over the centuries. I suppose this idea of universal equality in the eyes of God could be considered radical, but it has always seemed perfectly logical and indisputable to me. After all, I always was taught that Jesus died for the sins of all humanity—not just Jews, not just gentiles, not just slaves or free, and certainly not just for men. Ironically enough, those whom I feel most supported and inspired by—Sister Amata, my mother, my father, my grandmother, my friend Father John, Saints Teresa and Catherine, Dorothy Day, and even the old women with the rosaries from my earliest memories of church—comprise a noticeably lopsided list. It is overwhelmingly female.

When I was in elementary school, my younger brother was allowed to serve at the altar during mass, but I was not. It hadn't really occurred to me before that some careers were reserved only for men. After a great debate in our diocese, girls were eventually allowed to serve at the altar. I accepted the decision happily, but from then on I was more acutely aware of gender distinctions in my church—most blatantly, there were no female deacons or priests, and the pronoun "he" was used countless times during mass, while "she" rarely, if ever, appeared. After mass each week, I assailed my mother with questions and began to feel a great strain between my inherited faith and the "radical" belief in the equality of men and women.

A few years later, my family traveled to a little village in the Dominican Republic with a group, where my father did dental work. I translated between patients and doctors, and my brother and mother told children Bible stories and taught them about basic preventive health care. Although my background in doctrinal Catholicism was limited, my faith life was fairly strong. My experience with "feminism," however, was already extensive.

One dark and balmy night, under a beautiful starry sky, my brother and I sat with a friend of ours who was preparing to enter the seminary. We were three lone Catholics among two dozen or so Christians of various Protestant denominations, and we eventually came upon the subject of the role of women in the church.

"Of course women should be included in the priesthood—it's just a matter of time!" I ventured when the subject was broached that evening. It hadn't even occurred to me that I was making any sort of bold statement.

Our friend, much older and more familiar with Catholic doctrine, grimaced and immediately shot back with age-old, traditional answers defending the current and static definition of priesthood. He asserted: "The priesthood has always been exclusively male because Jesus chose twelve men as his disciples. I mean, who are we to contradict Jesus? Who are we to impose the values and ideas of our modern, more egalitarian society, such as feminism, upon Jesus' perfection? We must trust that he knew what he was doing—he was God, after all, and his decisions clearly were meant to transcend time and shifting cultures."

His reasons didn't satisfy me in the least and instead upset me even more. In the pit of my stomach, I felt conflicted. I was still convinced that the Jesus I had come to know would never have endorsed the discrimination against women our church has been practicing for centuries.

Tears began to well up in my eyes, but I fought hard to keep them there. After all, I didn't want to play any further into my friend's stereotypes of all women being overly emotional. Still, I felt hurt—what my friend was claiming seemed to completely contradict the very church that I had come to know and love. And although the whole conversation had been disturbing already, it was what happened next that hurt me the most.

Calmly, our friend decided to appeal to my brother, as another rational man. Until this point, even the controversy over serving at the altar had failed to convince me that there was anything intrinsically better about my brother simply because of his maleness. I like to think that part of what occurred next could be attributed to the young age of my brother and his desire to be part of something that privileged him.

"What do you think, Mike?" our friend asked.

"I guess that makes sense. I mean, the Gospels do say that Jesus chose twelve male disciples to be with him at the last supper. And Jesus was perfect."

"Exactly!" my friend affirmed quickly and excitedly.

I felt betrayed and was struck speechless. I stopped listening as our friend continued with his weak defense of the traditional definition of priesthood. I knew in my heart that there were faults in the logic being employed. But it saddened me more that my brother, generally an independent thinker, had allowed the church's "authority" to trump his own reason and conscience. My subsequent plea that night was emotional and instinctual. When we returned to the United States, however, I resolved to investigate the issue myself.

*

By the end of my sophomore year in college, I had completely abandoned my chemistry studies in lieu of a theology major. I eventually dug for information regarding the role of women in the church. Sure enough, I found plenty that challenged the conception of the priesthood offered by my seminarian friend years earlier. My brother, too, took the time to explore the history of the church and came to similar conclusions.

I believe passionately that there is something mysterious and sacred about the Roman Catholic Church that has kept it alive through centuries of tragedy and corruption, and that the church also has a huge capacity, and also a great necessity, for constant renewal. But I also worry about the welfare and vitality of the church. I am saddened by the widespread definition of the church as an institution, both by defenders of the church and its opponents. Each day I face this growing question: how can and should I be involved in the changes that must take place?

On one hand, it is important to learn to follow the little way of St. Therésè of Lisieux—doing everything, however small, for God without too much unproductive worry about the monumental changes that must take place. But on most days, I also feel called to be part of the reformation! Time and again I have been warned that if I cry out too loudly or publicly, if I dare make waves or ask too many questions, I won't be welcomed fully as a member of the church anymore.

I look to my community of mentors—St. Teresa of Ávila, St. Catherine of Siena, and Dorothy Day—and I pray for some measure of their patience, courage, creativity, and persistence. I often return to the articles written about Sister Amata, and each time, I find among the articles a worn photograph of myself gazing up at her in her beautiful scarlet cape. Her own eyes glimmer with great joy. As I stare lovingly at the picture, I pray that she is watching over me, cheering me on from heaven as I struggle with these difficult questions about the church. I imagine her giggling at my attempts to make lumpy applesauce as she taught me, and taking great pride as I create new masterpieces from construction paper to be displayed on the bulletin boards of my classroom. As my life continues on its winding path, I pray that I will find new ways to garner strength from the ambiguities of the church. I pray that I am able to remain attentive to and appreciative of the Holy Spirit at work in my life as teacher, mentor, and counselor to high school students each day. I pray to be at peace with an imperfect and, above all else, human church while trusting that God will work through me and the rest of its members to continue to bring about the Kingdom of God on earth.

In Search of Community

DISCUSSION QUESTIONS

1. How important is it for you to feel connected to a community? Why?
2. What kinds of communities are you a part of? For each community you identify: Who participates? Where do you meet? What do you talk about? What rituals are part of your time together? How would this community define or identify itself? What does this community offer to you? What do you offer to the community?
3. How do these communities support your feminism? How do these communities support your faith?
4. Are you a part of any communities that make it difficult for you to honor your faith? Are you part of any communities that make it difficult for you to honor your feminism?
5. What communities would you like to discover that would support you in your search for a feminist faith? Do you know if any such communities already exist in your region?

VISIONING ACTIVITIES

Imagine a supportive community that would encourage your personal growth for the individual you are right now.

1. Who is a part of this community? Is it exclusive or limited in some way? Do you know some people you would like to invite to be a part of this community? What interests or skills would you like people in your community to possess?
2. Where do you gather? How does your gathering place support the needs of the community? Would you add any particular materials to your space? Imagine what the space looks like. Draw it or describe it in writing, using sensory details.

3. When do you gather? How often do you gather? How would you fit this community into your schedule? Could you add this community without letting go of another commitment? What commitments would you be willing to let go of in order to participate in this community?

4. Why does your group gather? What concerns, commitments, ideas, or beliefs are central for you? What do you talk about?

5. What would happen at your gatherings? Would there be repeated rituals that would take place during each meeting? What responsibilities would members of the community have? What would the leadership be like?

6. What sorts of resources would help you build this community? What people in your life would be available to help and advise you? Which existing communities inspire you?

7. How does your community interact with the wider culture and its institutions?

"How am I creative?" Claire asks.

"All of the curriculum you wrote when you were teaching is certainly creative!" Rachel responds immediately.

Claire grins sheepishly, "Oh, I hadn't thought about that."

It is easy for us to forget that we are all blessed with creativity. For Rachel, creativity is a way of life. Her home-based studio is a whirl of activity. There are always stories to write, objects to invent, gifts to make. She applies her creativity to new ways of imagining God and spiritual community as well. Claire also uses imagination to encourage her religion students to understand how faith influences life.

Indeed, it is creativity that enables us to continue hoping for a better future. Human flexibility and creativity are what change the world. Sometimes, we just need to remind each other that we possess this God-given gift.

Twelve

LOVED INTO THE EDGES OF MYSELF

Carol Brorsen

The invitation on the wall of the Kerby Lane coffee house said, "Art & Contemplative Prayer." As I scanned the words, "Come explore . . . in community . . . Thomas Merton . . . pastels," my eyes widened. I gently took one of the blue brochures.

"Wow," I said only half out loud to myself. I'd been exploring both art and silent meditation separately, by myself. Now, here was a group of people who had put the two together.

"I have to come up with a reason to move here," I decided then and there.

"Here," was Austin, Texas. I was visiting the city for the first time the day I found the flyer. I fell in love hard on that trip. From the first sight of the hills, the taste of the tex-mex cooking, the sound of the rockabilly bands, Austin became like a lover to whom I just had to return.

In Texas, Austin is an island of progressiveness. It's a great place for creative misfits from the region to go to start a band, create a tech business, or launch a grassroots uprising. There's an annual Spam-a-Rama, live music every night of the week somewhere, and women are allowed to swim and sunbathe topless at the city's natural springs swimming hole.

It would be two years before I loaded up a van and drove all my worldly possessions (okay, except for that closet full of stuff back at my parents' house on the farm in Oklahoma) to the promised land of Austin.

First I had to finish up my work in Lubbock, Texas, where I was working at a campus ministry leading small groups and organizing worship services and retreats with college students— trying desperately to obey God as I understood "him." There can be something intoxicating about being young, recklessly abandoned to an unexamined faith you'd stake your very life on, all while giving up the hard work of claiming your own desires and dreams to obey something bigger, something outside of yourself.

At the time, my aunt wondered aloud to my mother, "Is it a cult?" In reality, it was just a bunch of Methodists in love with Jesus. She was suspicious, though, because I had left my first real job out of college as a newspaper reporter in Oklahoma to move to Lubbock. Going to work there in the West Texas flatlands seemed to me to be the stuff of Old Testament nomads and New Testament missionaries. The whole "take up your cross and follow me" gig. I wanted to spend my life in some way that mattered. And yet, in looking back, I wonder if there was also something else at work. I wonder if I ran so furiously into the arms of God so that I could run away from myself—as if I tried to smother myself in God, in hopes that my secrets could be buried and smothered right along with me.

When I did finally make it to Austin, I rented a fabulous little shack near Lake Travis, just a short walk to the river. My front yard turned into a field where deer ambled at dusk, where wildflowers took over in spring, and where I would spend many nights watching stars and talking to God.

The evening I signed my lease, I went to a nearby outdoor restaurant on the lake, drank a margarita, and danced with a crowd of my new beloved Austinites as the band played. Then we watched the sun set, and I clapped right along with everyone else as soon as the last sliver of light sunk into the water. I felt free and hopeful.

A few days later, while unpacking and nesting, I opened a file made many years before labeled, "Art & Spirituality." Inside was the flyer I'd found two years before at the coffeehouse. I'd totally forgotten about it. Soon I'd made a copy of it, jotted a note, and mailed it off to the address listed. A couple of days later, a woman named Kathy called sounding a bit incredulous.

"That's just so strange," she said.

"Yeah, I've kept it for a couple of years," I said.

"Well, there's that. But what's even more incredible is that I'm offering this group again for the first time since then, and it starts in two weeks."

Silence hung between us while that news sunk in.

"Would you like to be part of it?" she asked.

"Oh, yeah. I think I better."

The synchronicity could not be ignored.

Kathy explained that our art and prayer class would be one of the classes offered through the Servant Leadership School and led by members from her church, an Episcopal community called St. Hildegard's, after the twelfth-century mystic, Hildegard of Bingen.

She invited me to join them for worship on Sunday, and we made plans to meet then.

"Great. I'll see you Sunday," I said, and then sat for a long time in the swelling amazement of what had just unfolded.

On Sunday afternoon, a little after four o'clock, I entered the church fellowship hall where St. Hildegard's met. There were four rows of chairs facing each other, and the handful of people gathered, mostly women, were sitting in silence. I hesitated, not knowing if I should go in or not. A beautiful woman in her early forties came to greet me in a whisper, "Welcome. We have twenty minutes of contemplative silence before we start the service. Come join us."

I sat in a back row and breathed into the silence. A deep gong ended our silent prayer and the group began to sing softly, "All shall be well. All shall be well. And all manner of things shall be well," the seven-hundred-year-old words of mystic Julian of Norwich.

At the break I met Kathy; she introduced me to the others, and we settled in for the service. After the priest gave the sermon, she invited all those gathered to share their reflections on what she had just offered and the readings and how it all wove together with their own lives. I was shocked at the depth, integrity, and wisdom of what people shared and was a little overwhelmed by the intimacy of it all. Looking at people during the songs and readings, listening to the details of people's lives and their faithful questions—there was no hiding here.

This community also used inclusive language for God. At St. Hildegard's, God wasn't just Father, and Jesus wasn't Lord of anything. God was mother, friend, creator, and passionate fire. Jesus was our brother in justice struggles with those at the margins, the Christ alive and empowering us at the eucharist, but not one who desired to be groveled to like a landowning lord or a triumphant king.

What was going on here? It was so new to me. I was drawn in, and yet didn't quite feel like this was really church. It was unlike anything I'd experienced before. No hymnbooks, no pews, it was unclear just who was in charge, and what was so wrong with calling God Father, anyway?

After the sharing and the passing of the peace, we gathered in a circle around a table for the eucharist. We sang and handed each other the bread and wine, and then, of all things, musical instruments were passed out, and the congregation danced around the altar to end the service. Everyone was having so much fun, was so uninhibited. I just couldn't get into it. It was one thing to dance on an outdoor patio with a live band after drinking a margarita, but in church? I felt shy and kept my eyes on the song sheet.

I wouldn't be back there for a while, I thought when I left. Still, I was looking forward to our art and prayer group.

Every Thursday night for ten weeks we gathered to eat, worship, and share from our experience of practicing daily contemplative prayer. I was by far the youngest in the group of all women. With great reverence, we heard each other's stories and marveled at the images that had emerged out of one another's prayer and life through the brilliant colors of pastels on paper. We were challenged to risk and were held with grace and compassion when we did. We talked about the struggles and joys in our lives, big and small, from relationships to hot flashes to the intimacies of our life with God.

At the first class, we were given a set of pastels and a huge spiral-bound set of pastel papers. That night I went home and sat on the floor with my new art supplies. I let myself simply pick colors I was drawn to. The process of praying as I pushed and pulled reds, oranges, and yellows across the burnt orange paper brought out passion and longing and anger and sadness that I didn't even know was in me. I was startled by the force of my emotions and the power of the orange pastel chalk under my hand as images of flames appeared on the paper. And then, I pressed so hard that I ripped a hole through the surface.

What a sign.

I think there is only so far we can go by ourselves, and then it gets too hard; we need a community to go on from there. I have this idea that there are parts of ourselves that are like geodes—those rocks with amazing crystals inside. They have hard surfaces, rough, heavy. We carry the rocks around inside us, and they feel like burdens. Sometimes it's too painful to open them ourselves, and often we don't realize that there might be something beautiful hiding in the unremarkable casement. There are times that we need someone else to take hammer and chisel and lovingly break open the seemingly worthless rocks, and then others still to pick up the pieces and help us see the beauty inside.

I became friends with many of the folks from St. Hildegard's. Over the next couple of years, in more classes at the Servant Leadership School and over coffee and supper and popcorn at the movies, we told stories from our lives and talked theology. I read a book Kathy loved by Sallie McFague, *Metaphorical Theology: Models of God in Religious Language*.[1] We debated if Jesus had died for our sins or just been killed for political reasons. We asked each other what made us come alive. And we laughed, a lot.

But there was one thing I wasn't laughing about yet. Inside I carried a terrible tension between what I most longed for and the Bible that I believed condemned my deepest passion. The truth of my life was that what made me come alive was women. I had known this for years, but thought maybe I could shake it. The last thing I wanted to be was a lesbian. I suspected my family would flip and my friends from my campus ministry days in Lubbock would not see my faith as credible anymore. Life in society itself wouldn't be a walk in the park. And worst of all, I feared that God would condemn me if I chose to disobey the Bible's "clear" word of "No" to my body's longings. I had to be strong and resist the temptations.

But I was running out of goodness, and my once sure and solid faith was starting to collapse. If this was it—struggle, obedience, misery—then my life was a cruel joke, dealt to me by the very hands of the God I once loved with every ounce of my strength. I stopped going to church altogether. I couldn't take it anymore. I wasn't sure this God could be trusted.

It got worse. One night I stood in the field near my house, shook my fist at the stars, and said, "Damn it! I liked believing in you." I used my hardcover Oxford Annotated Bible with Apocrypha to hold my bedroom window open and didn't bother to move it when it rained. I dreamed that a tornado was destroying the church in my hometown where I grew up.

When you throw your whole worldview out the window, it can be hard to get out of bed in the morning. And for a while, it was. Kathy could tell I was in deep. She called me every morning at 9 A.M. for a couple of months.

During this time, I read a quotation that Rainer Maria Rilke had written in *Letters to a Young Poet.* This became my transitional theology:

> Have patience with everything unresolved in your heart and try to love the questions themselves as if they were locked rooms or books written in a very foreign language. Don't search for the answers, which could not be given to you now, because you would not be able to live them. And the point is to live everything. Live the questions now. Perhaps then, someday far in the future, you will gradually, without even noticing it, live your way into the answer.[2]

I had plenty of questions. What if my whole life up to this point had been a crock? What if giving up what you love isn't what God asks of us? What if sacrifice and obedience isn't the ultimate goal of our lives with God? What if living out of love is more important than fear? What if I'm just being deceived?

I didn't have any clear guides for this new path and I wasn't willing to talk about it enough to really find any. I was silenced by shame. I would have to listen to the Spirit and her whispers to me. I would have to listen to my body, to my intuition. And I knew somehow, I couldn't do it all by myself.

In the midst of all the pain of having my beliefs shaken to the core, I kept signing up for new Servant Leadership classes: poetry and storytelling in the Bible, a class on encountering Jesus through iconography and meditation. I went partly for the supper, partly because I liked being with my friends at St. Hildegard's who loved me in the midst of my funk and critical spiritual questions, and partly because I still had a shred of hope that some piece of God could be salvaged out of the wreckage of my former religious beliefs.

Most of my friends at St. Hildegard's had experienced dark nights of the soul and lived to tell about it, I had heard their stories. I wasn't sure I could trust God, but I began to believe I could trust them with all of myself. I couldn't pray anymore, but they could pray for me. I wasn't sure of God's love, but they loved me, this I knew. Not because the Bible told me so, but because I experienced it.

One week, Kathy told me she was offering the homily that Sunday and invited me to come hear her. I went. At the eucharist, as we stood around the table, I looked from face to face and realized that I was in the midst of my community. I knew these people and I loved them. They were my community whether I knew it or not, even whether I liked it or not. I went back the next Sunday, and the next, and the next. I still wasn't sure about God, but I found enough glimpses of God there—in the midst of hugs and honest prayers and the stories that people told from their lives—enough to give me hope. I had found a place where I could be my most authentic self and where I knew I was loved.

I later learned that, like the first pastel of flames I drew, Hildegard often used metaphors of fire in her writing and art. Fire as primal. Fire as the breath of life. Fire as God. I may be imposing myself into her nine-hundred-year-old creations, but I like to read into her images ways our bodies connect with the Sacred. I like to think that she was touching on these interweaving threads of Spirit, nature, sexual energy, and God, maybe even without meaning to, or knowing it, when she saw visions of a divine figure of Love, Wisdom, and Power who said things like

> *I am the fiery life of divine substance,*
> *I blaze above the beauty of the fields,*
> *I shine in the waters,*
> *I burn in sun, moon, and stars.*
> *And I awaken all to life.*[3]

In the midst of the community of St. Hildegard's, I was able to recognize the ways Love had been speaking to me all along. In this community, I was awakened to life. Through the fiery and hilarious lives of the members of St. Hildegard's, I was loved into the edges of myself. God held me through them when I broke open and then showed me the beauty of the blazing life inside. Eventually, I did find the courage and the theology to really come out. I brought my girlfriend to church. And one Sunday, I finally laid down my cross, took up a tambourine, and danced around the altar.

Thirteen

S P I R I T U A L   T A P E S T R Y

Monica Ann Maestras

✝

*I*f I could turn my faith into something tangible for you to hold, I might hand you an unfinished quilt. It would be a patchwork of Catholicism, astrology, and bits and pieces of other religions as I learn more about them, like the religion of my Mayan and Aztec ancestors. I have chosen to blend so many faiths to express my spirituality because I strongly believe that there is no one "right" or "chosen" religion or deity. In my eyes religions are all just different types of maps to guide us through this life as moral beings. I see all deities as being equal because they are actually the same source of higher power or spiritual oneness that is interpreted differently by different cultures. A working-class Chicano family in the United States shaped my identity, so naturally I was raised Catholic, and my native deity is God. Catholicism is generally considered to be a patriarchal religion, but I have been able to reconcile my religious beliefs with my strong feminist values by paying special homage to the Virgin Mary as a strong feminine figure within my religion. In this way I have created my own special blend of spirituality, and I believe my acceptance of many faiths has given me a wider worldview.

I choose to continue practicing Catholicism as an adult because I feel a sacred connection with its rituals. In church I love to sing the familiar hymns in Spanish and let the words *Padre, Dios, paz,* and *cielo* roll off my tongue. It is the only time I confidently can speak my native language without embarrassment from not knowing what the words mean. As we start to say my favorite prayer, the "Our Father," I reach for the hand of the stranger next to me, and he does the same to his neighbor and so on until the entire church is bound together in prayer. It is the only time I am not afraid when a stranger reaches to touch me in public, and that makes me feel safe.

The best part is the eucharist. I anticipate communion with thirst and hunger for wholeness and community. The priest prepares the host and wine, and chants, *"Through him, with him, in him, in the unity of the Holy Spirit."* I respond aloud, with the rest of the congregation, *"Lord, I am not worthy to receive you, but only say the word and I shall be healed."* Then I stand in line, and at last it is my turn. I cup my hands before a eucharistic minister and receive the host, the body of Christ. I turn to another minister who hands me the cup of wine, the blood of Christ. As I sip the watered-down white zinfandel, it washes the thin wafer from the roof of my mouth to make a nourishing paste, and I am healed.

✳

I naturally feel this same connection with the Mayan religion because the Mayans are my ancestors. There is something to be said for the visceral experience of going back to the land of one's ancestors and feeling a spiritual connection. I experienced this when I visited Chichen Itza, which is a Mayan ruin site in the Yucatan Peninsula of Mexico. I was taken aback by the strong and eerie presence I felt when I walked into the ruins. I stood in a room that used to be a classroom and reached down to touch the dirt that was so soft and fine that it seemed to be sifted. I ran my hands over the bone-colored stones and thought of the people who put them there—people who looked like me, with shiny black hair and rich skin that is smooth and dark like coffee beans. I started to cry and stood silent, letting myself be surrounded by the dense thick air that seemed to ground me until I felt akin to a tree both planted in the earth and branching out into the heavens. That is also how I see my spirituality: as a tree whose roots are planted in the history and culture of my people, with its branches reaching out in different directions to collect strength from other sources.

I later came to learn more about the religion of my ancestors when I read a book about the Aztec religion, which grew out of the Mayan religion. I identified with their religion because they had no concept in their culture of one god or one part of nature being dominant over all others. This conviction resonates with my belief in the equality of religions. From the beginning, from their creation, the Aztecs started with two gods, a man and a woman, Omecihuatl and Ometecuhtli, the God and Goddess of Duality. Duality was an important aspect of the Aztec's concept of nature. Instead of four seasons there were two: dry and rainy.

The Aztec calendar was created by bringing together two calendars: the solar and lunar. The solar calendar was thought of as the masculine calendar, marking specific natural events, like equinoxes and solstices, and defining how they related to agriculture. The lunar calendar was thought of as the feminine calendar because it comprised 260 days, exactly the same time period as human gestation. Related rituals were performed at times marked by the cycles of the moon. I love that the Aztecs worshiped the moon as a symbol of the life-giving power of women. That kind of worship feels familiar because I watch the moon's cycles and pay attention to how they affect my moods and emotions. At full moon I feel that all of my emotions and thoughts are right on the surface and seem drawn outward. I feel heavy and explosive with all of the tension. My favorite phase is the quarter moon, though. I am fascinated when I look up in the night sky and see a brilliant sliver juxtaposed to a shadow of all that is not seen. I become recharged and energized with all of its possibilities. The moon reconnects me with the awesome excitement of all there is to learn and experience.

As much as I respect the moon, I have an even stronger affinity for the sun because it is my astrological "planet." Each astrological symbol has its own related planet, but I am a Leo, and my "planet" is the star at the center of the solar system. I identify with astrology because it, too, honors and respects different forms of human nature with the twelve zodiac signs. Astrology to me is *like* a religion in that it sets a path to follow with horoscopes and planetary guides. Astrology reminds me of how the Mayans and Aztecs carefully studied the paths of the sun and the moon to guide their daily decisions. I can relate to worshiping the sun because I feel there is something about the sun that guides and nourishes me.

I practice astrology by reading my daily horoscope online and listening to planetary guides on the radio, and I consider these sources when I make decisions throughout the day. For instance, if my horoscope tells me there is a high chance for conflict today and the planetary guide reports that Mercury is in retrograde, which usually affects communication, I know to take my time in communicating with people and try to head off any conflict that may be caused by miscommunication. This guides me in a similar way to that in which a sermon in mass does. If the priest addresses being more forgiving and gives the example of Jesus forgiving his own persecutors, I know there is a reason for me to be there and to hear that sermon. I will consider that message in my relationships for the coming week.

Aside from using astrology as a guideline in life, I have a strong sense of connection with my astrological sign. Leos are fire signs and considered to be leaders who are generous, vain, and very passionate. I find strength in recognizing in myself generosity and leadership abilities, and I identify with being a fire sign because I am a very passionate, vocal person. I identify so strongly with my sign that I have a tattoo of the astrological symbol for Leo on my left arm. I chose a bold red circle with a black outline to encompass the symbol. The symbol looks like a snake curved to represent the shape of a lion's mane. My tattoo is not on the small of my back or on my ankle where it can be hidden. I placed it on the outside of my upper left arm where it can be seen all summer long and warmed by the sun.

❖

Another source of strength within my spirituality is in my veneration of the Virgin Mary. The Mexican/Hispanic culture in which I was raised embraces her as a powerful religious icon worthy of honor and adoration. Thinking of her, I find added strength and pride in being a woman, and I find unity and balance within my own personal spirituality. As much as I believe in God and Jesus and the Holy Spirit, I trust the Holy Mother, the Virgin Mary. She is the centerpiece of my Latina flavor of Catholicism. I have spent my most crucial and memorable moments of prayer kneeling before her. As a second grader at Sacred Heart Elementary School, I prayed every day after school at the Santuario. I stared up at the granite statue of the Holy Mother encased in glass and surrounded by brick, flowers, and molten candles, and wished desperately for my stepfather to stop abusing me and for my mother never to find out. At our wedding, my husband and I knelt before a lifelike mahogany carving of the Virgin Mary and prayed for the first time as a married couple. Even now I am calmed by the scent of wax and roses when I stop after mass to light a candle and say a prayer to my Holy Mother.

I also identify with the Virgin Mary as a symbol of my faith because I love that her life-giving power is so respected within my culture, and the images of her I have seen reflect the features of my people. I gaze upon the images of the Holy Mother, and I see myself and what I long to be. I see her flawless brown skin, her wavy black hair, and her intent eyes emanating the unconditional love and strength of a mother. In my bedroom above my dresser is a painting of the Virgin Mary and her baby, Jesus, whom she holds close to her chest as he sleeps peacefully. She is turned sideways and her rapt gaze is toward the heavens. Her deep blue shawl encircles the baby dressed in white swaddling clothes, and he is clinging to her with a tiny fist clenched around her robe. She wears a golden cloak around her head that illuminates her sweet face donned with a look of peaceful compassion. In front of this image, I pray for strength and hope for the miracle of life to be my own.

❁

Symbols of my spirituality are an important part of my faith as a contemporary woman. Around my neck I wear a silver necklace with three pendants that I have received as gifts from my family over the years. The first pendant is a double-sided oval of silver over bronze metal. On one side of the medal is the *Virgin de Guadalupe,* the patron saint of Mexico whose image is based on sightings of the Virgin Mary by an Aztec man named Juan Diego in Mexico City in 1531. On the other side of the medal is *El Nino de Atocha,* the patron saint of those who are imprisoned or victims of crime, whose image is based on an apparition of Jesus Christ as a boy that appeared in Atocha, Spain, to help a group of imprisoned Christians in the 1400s. The second pendant is a silver, handmade Leo symbol, and the third is a malachite-studded silver cross. These symbols of my faith are layered over my heart. As the pendants jingle with my movement, they remind me of the importance of equality by reflecting my beliefs that are different but equal. I wear them together to represent the myriad diverse beliefs that I hold and to remind me to remain open to the many different threads I continue to weave into my spiritual tapestry.

Fourteen

A COUPLE OF FEMINISTS

Adam J. Copeland and Megan J. Thorvilson

Throughout this essay, Megan Thorvilson's words appear in Roman text and Adam Copeland's in Italics.

I'm Lutheran. *I'm Presbyterian.* I'm from a town of fifty in rural North Dakota. *I'm from a big city in Florida.* I rarely eat meat and when I do, it's chicken. *I'm a carnivore—a meal without meat isn't worth eating.* We come from two different worlds, but we've dated for more than two years.

Throughout our relationship, I have changed immensely, coming to terms with who I am as a female child of God. On one of our first dates, in an effort to determine my political and religious persuasion, you asked me innocently over dessert, "Is the man the head of the household?" Without hesitating I exclaimed,

"Yes." Your jaw dropped. My stomach seized with nerves. My answer was meant to affirm your role in our new relationship. As I thought back on the male figures in my life, each claimed his identity through authority. As I grew up, nobody questioned the conventions of my town: at home, men ruled.

I had never considered dating a girl who was so conservative. In fact, I did not know anyone who advocated that men should be heads of households. I knew I could not be comfortable in a relationship that had inequality at its foundation. I wondered if our relationship would ever work.

Since you had just refused my offer to buy supper, I was quite surprised you thought as you did. I tried to understand your shock and reconcile that with your actions—you always opened the car door for me, you always paid for our meals, you never walked through a door before me. You made me feel like I was a delicate person to be provided for, but that was contrary to your understanding of male-female relationships.

Though I'm a feminist, I'm also a traditionalist. In the South where I grew up, respect for women is very important. Traditional values like paying for the meal if you ask someone out and opening doors for women are the norm. And in the beginning, since you hadn't been on many dates before, I thought it might be nice to drive since you did offer me the keys. These were ways I could demonstrate that I thought you were someone special. Though I have these traditional habits, I'd still call myself a feminist because I believe that equality should be the foundation of relationships between men and women.

Where I grew up, feminists were thought of as bra-burning, not-shaving, nonconformist, man-hating, ultraliberals. I was not and shall never be that type of feminist. That type of feminist (God bless them) would never fit in at home. I don't think anyone like that has ever driven through my town, let alone stayed to talk to anyone. You have to remember, people at home are scared of feminism because they associate it with only one kind of person—one too different to ever fit in, one suggesting more change than we can muster in the next fifty years. Since I was only exposed to that one stereotype about what it meant to be a feminist, I certainly did not consider myself a feminist when I left home for college.

It never occurred to me that you might not understand feminism as I did, since in my family and faith community, gender equality was considered the norm. Until I met you, I assumed all female collegiates had comparable views of feminism to those of my friends back home. For me, feminism involves equal rights for men and women, understanding that neither man nor woman is the head of the other, recognizing that our society has subordinated and still does subordinate women, working to change this pattern of subordination, and searching for an appropriate balance in relationships that honors the particular gifts of individual men and women. That conversation on our first date opened my eyes to the fact that not everyone understands feminism in the same way.

Ironically, it has been my relationship with you that has helped me to understand my own feminism. As we have dated, your more liberal views have slowly shaped my more conservative ones. A few years ago, I would not have been able to articulate what it meant to be a feminist Christian. Now, if you were to ask, I would tell you that I'm Megan Joy Thorvilson, a child of God. Part of my identity has been decided by my two x-chromosomes. I am female and though I wanted to be a boy when I was younger, I would never change my gender now. I love who I am and I want society to love me as well, but I want to define myself. I will not give that responsibility to society. I refuse to conform to the world's standards, while at the same time, I recognize myself as part of the world, a member of society with a responsibility to help change it. This change requires imagination and breaking down many boundaries that separate us from the truth that men and women are equal. I'm Megan Joy Thorvilson; I can't help but be me.

And I can't help being me. I'm Adam John Copeland, a child of God. I am a Christian and a feminist man. As a white, middle-class male, I recognize that I was born into a position of privilege in this society. Yet I also recognize that, from this position, I can work for the equality of men and women. Like you, I look to make changes within our warped society. I hate society's assumptions about gender, and I want to help us move forward. It's a big task since sexism runs so deep in our culture, yet it can start within our own relationship, as we strive to relate to each other as equals, both created by God to be ourselves.

We experienced an amusing but telling example of how people in my family believe that men are to be the head of women the first time you visited my family's farm in North Dakota. As we got ready to go out for the night, my parents said, "Now Adam, you're welcome to drive our car." They spoke in a tone that conveyed a necessity for you to drive. The fact that my farm is ten miles away from a paved road and you had no experience driving on the narrow gravel tracks had no bearing on the matter. It was clearly safer for me to drive, but in my parents' eyes, that wasn't the issue. I was the girl, you were the guy. In North Dakota, men drive.

This was a quick lesson in the fact that your family didn't share your feminist views, but since this was my first visit, I wasn't about to explain to your father that you and I had different strengths. Even though driving has nothing to do with gender, and you certainly are the better driver on gravel, I took the keys from your father. Maybe I should have said something to your father about my belief in gender equality. But since I barely knew him, I was afraid that he wouldn't have stayed around to listen had I brought up my true feelings. The fight for true equality must be taken at a realistic pace, and as our relationship has demonstrated, sometimes change can be realized best through relationships with those we care about. Maybe someday, as he watches the two of us interact, your father will change his views on how women and men are to relate to each other

in a household. And hopefully someday, I will be in a similar situa-
tion and will be able to act on my convictions, speaking up in the
face of sexism and gender inequality.

Though I think I would have agreed with your understanding of feminism even in high school, I never would have had the
courage to say so. And now, though I'm comfortable enough to
write for a book on feminism and faith, I wouldn't be comfortable reading this essay in my hometown. Feminism is its own "f"
word; we just would rather not mention it.

I brought my small town North Dakota worldview with me
when I attended St. Olaf College in Northfield, Minnesota. For a
time at St. Olaf, I tried to force that worldview on my new college
community. When I learned that St. Olaf didn't function in this
manner, I clung even tighter to my home ways. Not until late in
my sophomore year did I think past my initial reaction of "different is bad" and consider that not all the world should emulate my
hometown. I still struggle to reconcile the contradictory messages
of home and St. Olaf. I still seek the balance between embracing
new ideas and clinging to my home values that helped make me
who I am today.

At the beginning of our relationship, we often struggled with
these two worlds. I noticed that you seemed to be a different person
when you were at home. At home, you said nothing when family
members sent offensive e-mails about homosexuality; you kept silent
your views on the Iraq war. Back at college, you tended to be progres-
sive, but you sometimes felt this was disloyal to your small town roots.
I particularly noticed this in relation to issues in the church. I wanted
for you what I am fortunate to have—an open forum for theological
discussions. At my house, theological discussions are an Olympic
sport. On Sunday afternoons, my family critiques every aspect of wor-
ship from the flowers to the flowery diction of hymns. I grew up in a
church very aware of inclusive language in liturgy. My pastor—who
also happens to be my Dad—makes a conscious choice to avoid refer-

ring to God in masculine terms. My early encounter with some types of feminist theology has definitely influenced my theology.

Some of my favorite discussions of ours center on the church. In my background, church was very important, but less for the theology than for the community. Rarely did my family discuss theological issues, for it was known what we thought and assumed that we would all think that way in the future. Not until late in college did I begin to wrestle with the topic of feminism and its relationship to the church, and then my discussions never took place at home.

I still feel lots of anxiety over progressive issues when I'm at home, church included. I'm scared to reveal my support for gays and lesbians in the church, my interest in interfaith dialogue, my understanding of evolution, and my approach to reading and interpreting the Bible. When some members of my family come to visit, we can't even talk about women being pastors. I feel like I have to conform to the beliefs of my family, church, and community. At home, everyone assumes a certain way of thinking that fails to leave room for other viewpoints. In college, I felt more comfortable disagreeing with those around me because of the open dialogue on many important issues.

It has been both difficult and inspiring to witness your struggle with tough issues that challenged the viewpoint you inherited from your family and faith community at home. Even though there are many theological conversations that are off-limits in your family, we have been able to have theological conversations, helping faith remain at the center of our relationship. On one particular Sunday that I'll never forget, Pastor Benson entered the sanctuary wearing his red stole. We were sitting beside each other in the pew and, growing up liturgically mindful, I knew that pastors only wear red stoles on one day of the year: Pentecost. I didn't expect anyone else to care about this random point of ecclesiastical fashion sense, but as soon as you saw Pastor Benson you gleefully noted, "It's Pentecost!"

There's no denying that we have similar liturgical interests. Worship has always been central to our relationship, and from that, our faith has grown together.

Faith supports our relationship. It's important that we turn to our faith rather than society for guidance. We don't answer to society; we answer to each other and to God. Feminism and Christianity complement each other, both recognizing our equality without eliminating our differences.

On our one-year anniversary there were no roses, expensive dinner, or champagne—my roommate thought we were crazy. Instead, we met each other for church as if it were any other Sunday. After church we walked to a nearby restaurant and exchanged prayers that we had written to thank God for our relationship. The prayers articulated our love for each other's individuality, our commitment to one another, and our equality before God. We continue to try to live out our relationship in both a Christian and feminist way.

In many ways we don't notice, feminism pervades every aspect of our relationship, including decision making. We treat each decision on its own terms and use discussion to lay out each of our interests in the situation. When we think about our future together, we weigh our individual ambitions against what is best for our relationship. Each of our voices must be heard equally as we struggle to balance our options and to do what is best for both of us as individuals and as a couple.

I continually struggle with whether we should operate as one unit or two individuals. Part of our individual identities encompasses the other, yet I never want a compromise to compromise either of our identities. It's a delicate balance, but our relationship thrives when that balance is maintained.

This balance might be the product of a healthy relationship between two Christian feminists that emphasizes trust, equality, and regard for each other. And the communication skills that serve our relationship also serve us well in our other relationships.

Let's face it, though—sometimes we're the ones needing the help. Once after a few months of dating, I tried to hide my visits to a tanning salon from you because I knew you think that this practice supports unhealthy standards for women. I had wanted to go so that I didn't look so ghostly white after the long winter. I told you after a few visits, and you calmly explained that you loved me just as I am. The discussion that followed my disclosure was difficult but worthwhile. Our mistakes are no reason to scream and freak out; through good (sometimes long) talks, we work out our problems.

It didn't take much convincing at all for us to pledge early in our relationship never to lie to each other, never to hang up on each other or refuse to communicate. It's amazing how far strong communication has taken us. Because you have never lied to me, I never wonder if our discussions are genuine—your word trumps all others.

Sometimes I forget that our level of communication is not the norm. When we first started dating, a friend from home beginning a new relationship could not believe how comfortably we discussed anything from my period to our faith. Once when she and I talked about the physical aspect of our relationships, I told her that we talked about everything before acting. In dismay, she exclaimed, "How can you talk about that?" It's not easy, but if we focus on the lasting benefit of communication rather than the immediate awkwardness, discussions are always well worth it.

It has taken plenty of work to keep our relationship healthy. Maybe that's why society seems so stuck. Discussions take time and effort—sometimes even prayer. Most positive societal changes are preceded by many conversations, but it usually takes years. The church is famous for this. For example, the Presbyterian Church didn't reunite after its separation over the issue of slavery until 1983. I'm the type of feminist who trusts that society can change, but change both requires and results in communication.

I now try to be very aware of the way feminism interacts with Christianity. Last year I graduated from St. Olaf and decided to enter seminary. I hope one day to be a Lutheran pastor. After only a year in seminary, I've learned that the Evangelical Lutheran Church in America (ELCA) and many local churches have plenty of problems in how they approach women in ministry as well as male-female relationships. I recently witnessed one example in a local church where I attended a wedding. The scripture reading for the service was from Ephesians 5: "Wives, be subject to your husbands as you are to the Lord. For the husband is the head of the wife just as Christ is the head of the church, the body of which he is the Savior. Just as the church is subject to Christ, so also wives ought to be, in everything, to their husbands."[1] Wow! May the world hear me say right now that whomever I marry will **not** be the head of me. This offensive passage exemplifies a negative pattern of male-female relationships. It does **not** describe a healthy relationship between two people. It does **not** highlight the gifts of the woman, but assumes her to be inferior to the man. It's **not** feminist.

The ELCA also has not yet fully accepted women. The Lutheran Church did not grant the right to ordain women until 1970. Since then women have struggled to find full standing as ministers in the church. Men dominate all the higher governing bodies of the ELCA. And, believe it or not, no woman has held our highest office of Presiding Bishop! In our churches, very few women serve as head pastors, while many women serve under male heads of staff. It is very sad that I still, from time to time, must explain to people that women can be ordained, that women have the skills to be pastors, that women are more than wives for men. I cannot imagine the hurt caused by churches that still fail to ordain women. These churches must change their narrow thinking about clergy and ordination, for the church needs good leadership, and women are out there eager to answer the call.

Like most large institutions, my denomination, the Presbyterian Church (USA), has plenty of work to do before we realize true equality between men and women. The national church has been blessed with several strong female Moderators; however, we cannot point to a few positive examples and sit and rest. The church cannot afford to wait. It is the duty of us all—including the men who are in power—to believe in our hearts and show forth in our lives that the potential for female leadership in the church remains unrealized.

So I'm Lutheran. *And I'm Presbyterian.* I'm from a town of fifty in rural North Dakota. *I'm from a big city in Florida.* I don't really like meat. *I do.*

TOGETHER WE ARE CHRISTIAN FEMINISTS, HOPING, PRAYING TO CHANGE THE WORLD.

Fifteen

The Wine-Like Properties of Orange Fanta

Sadie Ackerman

Shortly after I stood before my congregation in an insanely ruffled yellow dress on Confirmation Sunday, I decided I was too smart for the whole thing. I quit youth group and church on Sunday mornings and spent the time, instead, documenting my own invented religion in a spiral bound notebook. It amazes me still how thorough—and how thoroughly sterile—the whole book was, as if faith could be heaved into existence by contriving a perfectly rationalized airtight box in which to seal it. My religion lacked a lot, not the least of which was community, so when I moved out, the notebook stayed at my parents' house in a box of other things I'd outgrown along the way.

At college, I once again took solace in the people and the ritual of my Protestant upbringing, eventually switching my major to religious studies. Still, in my own academic way, I continued to try to outsmart religion, to find that one misunderstood phrase in the Latin Vulgate that would prove I had been right all along in not buying the whole package. I was bound and determined to find that one thing that didn't quite fit and start a revolution. In the meantime, I tried to devise ways to make myself comfortable with modern Christianity. I joined the leadership team of the university ministry group and taught senior high Sunday school. When a group from my church went to Central America to host youth summer camps for the children there, I went along and then led the team that went the following year.

Ultimately, this mission work is what saved me. It's hard to take tortillas and orange Fanta for communion in a dirt-floored church with chickens wandering in and out and still not be able to think outside the box just a little bit. In the jungles of a developing country, it became not only necessary to isolate the essence of Christianity for myself, but it became part of my assignment, my responsibility to the outside world to do so for others. So I began to shake off the damage that years of bad Sunday school art had done to my faith: a pale Mary jumped off her pastel-clad poster and left that clean little scene behind her. She would've had much more in common with these brown shoeless girls, too essential to their families—some with children of their own strapped to their backs—to come to the camp we'd planned for thirteen- to fifteen-year-olds. The draw of a soda machine and foosball table in the youth room back home suddenly seemed as irrelevant as it had been all along to the substance of what my religion had to offer. I learned that I wasn't a Christian . . . I was an *American* Christian, and that some of what had disappointed me about the church wasn't Christian in that sense either.

Of course, having stripped away as many of the American constructs surrounding Christianity as I could, I was compelled to consider old European constructs and those of ancient Judaism, as well. I felt I must approach the text knowing not only

ancient Greek, but also ancient impulses. But how much historical and cultural context could I be expected to take into account
exactly? How far back did I need to go? I went as far as I could as
an undergraduate, but it never felt sufficient. I could spread my
notes and books out on a table and argue just about any point
handed to me, but I found that my research mainly served to bolster my own conclusions, not to determine them. What moved
me and changed me were the mysteries, the realities that could be
only partially articulated. They could be argued and described,
but never captured; they were like music or breath or water.

In retrospect, I understand that much of my own tension
with the church as a feminist came, ironically, from my accessing
it through a masculine model. My disappointment stemmed
from my own knee-jerk reaction to don a three-piece power suit
and kick some ass in some administrative office room somewhere, not to prove I could be a man's equal, but to prove I could
actually *be* a man, and possibly even better than he could. This
was the very critical task of my mother's generation, those
boomer-brand feminists who worked so hard to change the social
structure and the laws and the very texts themselves. Those of us
who are their daughters, however, have had the luxury of a different task. We are redetermining the femininity they had to set
aside to make their strides, reclaiming words like guidance, encouragement, intuition.

As a mother of two young children, I don't always have the
time to run through a degree's worth of biblical theology, history,
and several ancient languages before a fifteen-minute morning
devotional. To be honest here, I don't even always have time for
the devotional itself, so these intuitive aspects of my faith are critical to overcoming tensions with the church in many ways, not
just as they relate to feminism.

A lot of people breathe, "Thank God!" when the stoplight finally turns green, but I'm one of those who feels actual indebted-
ness. I get the wind knocked out of me daily by the splendor of a

fallen leaf or the translucence of the skin across my son's temple. My first religious experience ever was that of pure beauty, in fact. I burst into tears in the kitchen while my father made me a peanut butter sandwich to take to kindergarten just because I saw the shadow of a butterfly cross behind a sheet of that tinted '70s glass with the little concentric circles all over. It blew my mind how beautiful the butterfly was even when partially obscured, how graciously unattainable its little silhouette was as it flitted away. It was my first experience of the way God would move in my world from then on.

Along the way, my studies have been important, *very* important. Yet an actual chronology of my spiritual journey reveals a sequence of mile markers that hardly even depend on literacy, let alone intellectualism. What I need from Christianity isn't always in the text or in the notes on the text or in the commentary on the notes on the text. Yet it suffuses the text, like the white shapes the black letters carve out all around themselves. It is the grainy-smooth stick of the page as it is turned. It is the way the corners curl. Sometimes the text enlightens one of those mile markers and greater knowledge deepens my understanding of its wisdom, but the it itself is almost always a quiet little secret wafting around in the air currents between heaven and earth.

This relationship, of course, demands a daily faith. How can I be sure that what I know is right? It is no simple thing. Being a recent newcomer to the social and religious climate of the South, where I've had friendships actually end over whether or not spanking is a biblical principle, I am well acquainted with self-doubt and the very fine line at which personal revelation becomes treachery to the dominant group. Admittedly, it would be easier to have tradition and a specific authority there to answer all my questions, but given that I was raised in a generation bestowed with the arrogance to know that tradition and authority can sometimes be wrong, that's just not enough for me. Once one crosses that presumptuous line, the path diverges: repent and return or forge ahead, believing personal enlightenment has divine purpose. There are times when I'm certain that God has fed and blessed my steps away from mainline theology. Other times I can't remember exactly what happened to lead me to that point; was it truly divine or merely my own flawed voice? It takes bravery to step back and stand alone, inviting direct experience, even demanding it, and then, more dramatically, depending on it when it is but a memory recalled.

But it's no special thing, really. I believe Christians all over do it every day. For most reasonable, intelligent people, there's bound to be some tension between their deeply held values and the church, whether the values are feminist, racial, sexual, or political in nature. Everyone must draw the line somewhere between the authority that resides externally and the one that can be individually claimed; we must each draw that line and then walk it like a tightrope perpetually.

For me, finding the line meant learning to let go of the intellectual arguments that are the bases of canon and of legislation and of doctrine and, even, of reformation. I had to learn to trust that the same deep current that feeds me is actually an underground river stretching back into ancient eras, the water that sustained my sisters—those simply referred to in the Bible by the phrase, "and other women," or not referred to at all. Sometimes power, true power, is so ubiquitous and so essential to its cause that it cannot be extricated from it.

Like women in church history, this kind of power is often not well recorded; its place is not fixed or maintained. Instead, it is a tradition of intuition and guidance. There is no evidence that Mary Magdalene, for instance, had any superior background or education, yet it was to her that Simon Peter came for encouragement. Peter, the Rock, widely considered to be a foundation of the Christian church, faltered after the crucifixion and went to Mary for comfort and guidance. There was no title waiting for her in that role, no papal-like line of succession that followed it.

However, imagine on your own what might have become of Peter, of all of us, if he had instead wandered away from Jerusalem discouraged and confused. And imagine what might have happened to me if I had read the text of Peter and not seen the white shape of Mary Magdalene cradling all around him.

That is not to say the very real shortcomings of ecclesiastical history are excused or that women aren't in need of some measure of political power. Christianity was not invented, perfected, and patented in 33 C.E., but developed by centuries' worth of people, all struggling to make sense of it in the same way we do today, giving its surface a shimmering, shifting sheen. Sometimes what the church appears to be and what it is underneath are not the same. Sometimes orange Fanta is a bottle of soda pop and sometimes it is the blood of Christ. We must learn to trust that distinction and to trust that the uncorrupted truth of Christianity still resides at its core and feeds us whether or not it is visible. We must learn to pray with mouths skyward, like fish who gulp in water, knowing that it is also air.

Sixteen

F O U N D   T H I N G S

Katie Haegele

Since I graduated from high school, I quit going to church, I got my wisdom teeth out, and I discovered found poetry. That's kind of a bare bones accounting for a whole ten years, but I mention those three things for a reason. They're more closely related than you may think.

The first thing you should know is that I put off getting the teeth out for a good ten years. When I was seventeen or so, my dentist took an X-ray and said that all four wisdom teeth—still sleeping inside my gums—should come out as soon as possible. No way, I thought, even as I smiled and nodded at him. If they ever started to hurt, I would deal with it then.

For a while the teeth remained quiet, and I thought I had outfoxed the dentist with my plan to ignore them and make them go away. But by the time I was in my twenties, they were in a rage.

Every few months the bottom two would undergo some seismic shift and start pressing against my gums, which throbbed with pain. They wanted out. Eventually they started coming in, but crazily—one of the bottom ones grew in sideways. When that tooth got infected, I had no choice but to make an appointment with an oral surgeon, who scolded me for waiting so long. "The recovery time is longer the older you are, and the risks are higher," he told me. "Why on earth did you let this get to this point?"

I couldn't tell him the truth—that, for some reason, somewhere along the line, my fear of getting my wisdom teeth out had gotten tangled up with my fear of death. Both were hazy, scary ideas in the un-pin-downable future, things I'd worried about until they'd become indistinguishable. It wasn't exactly that I was afraid I would die under the anesthesia, although at times my fear-addled brain latched onto that possibility, along with the idea that anything could happen to me while I was unconscious. It was something more like this: I was afraid of how much like death it would be. I'd be as vulnerable as a corpse there in the dentist's chair, deep in some unknowable black sleep. If I wasn't awake to be on guard, I'd be defenseless, helpless, totally unprotected. Mortal.

❖

This general faithlessness, this feeling that I was the only one looking out for me, had been a problem long before the teeth ever were. I was raised Catholic and grew up in a mostly Irish American enclave in an old suburb of Philadelphia—which, if you don't know, is about as Catholic as it gets.

Our community, close-knit and insular, had managed to remain fustily true to the old ways as though the world outside didn't exist. We lived in a huge metropolitan area on the East Coast, but none of the kids at Immaculate Conception knew anyone who wasn't Catholic; I'll bet most of their parents didn't, either. Several families in the parish had ten, eleven, twelve kids. Every weekend a group from our parish gathered in front of the local hospital to protest the hospital's practice of performing abortions.

On the first Friday of every month, the nuns trooped us in two straight lines, like the French girls from the *Madeline* books, from our squat little yellow-brick school building to the stony gothicness of the church next door, which was always chilly, even in the summer.

It's not easy being the odd one out in a group like this, but that's what I was. Odd. The other girls in my class were lovely and serene, like the sweet-faced Maria Goretti's and Saint Cecelia's in my mom's copy of *Lives of the Saints*. I, on the other hand, had as much energy as the boys and got better grades than all of them (except for Robert and Richard, my two main rivals).

My mom kept my fine hair embarrassingly short because she said I carried on too much when she tried to get out the tangles. I was sleepless at night and wild during the day, and when I grew up I wanted to be a famous novelist, a famous journalist, or a famous poet. But worse than the bad things about me that everyone could see were the things only I knew about. I wasn't good or holy the way I dearly wished to be. I couldn't even pray.

Oh, I was happy enough to chime in with everyone else when we said rote prayers in church or before school each morning, mostly because it seemed more like exercise or homework than something to do with God. It was the time set aside for silent, personal prayer that unnerved me. If I said the prayers inside my head, how was that different from plain old thinking? Did that mean God could hear all my thoughts? If so, I was in trouble. As I got older, the idea of having a conversation with someone who was invisible started to feel like magical thinking, no different from the dreamlike images from the Old Testament that, over time, our teachers gently told us probably didn't really happen. There was never any flood so big that it swept the whole earth after all. I still remember the look my parents exchanged over the dinner table when I brought home a religion quiz with only one true/false question marked wrong. Prayer is a two-way dialogue with God, the quiz had posited. False, I'd responded. I was good at taking tests, and I knew what they were driving at with that question, but I just couldn't give the answer they wanted. Prayer was not two-way. At least, it never had been for me.

My one salvation, if you'll pardon the expression, was the homily. During mass the priest gave a talk that was a reflection on that week's gospel reading; it was the only part of the mass that was different from week to week, the part that really came alive. I became fixated on the idea that I could write homilies, too. It would be like writing essays for school, only better, because you could stand up and share the things you'd figured out while you had been bent over your notebook, scribbling down the ideas that were burning inside you.

When I was around ten years old, a visiting priest came to our school, and we all filed down to the cafeteria, which we also used for assemblies, to listen to him talk about vocations. Some of us might hear a calling to the religious life someday, he said, so we should all listen carefully. Boys would be called to be priests or brothers; girls could be nuns. *Bleh*, I thought. Our nuns were scolding, gray-faced taskmasters who never, ever liked me. The only other kind of nun you could be was cloistered, shut away forever under a medieval vow of silence. Intellectually I already knew I wouldn't be called to the life of pious scholarship I wanted for myself; now I knew it in a way that hurt.

With all these dialogues and callings that were supposed to be going on, it was awfully quiet inside my head. And at some point, even my confidence in my answer to the true/false question began to waver. What if God did respond to people's thoughts, questions, and hopes—just not to mine? I spent a lot of time fidgeting around in my pew, worrying, faking it, looking around at my more content classmates and feeling lonely. Each time I tried to turn my thoughts to prayer, a mental breeze picked them up and blew them somewhere else, like a feather or an autumn leaf. Quite literally, I was at a loss for words.

❋

The minute I got out of my parents' house I stopped going to church, my old dream of writing homilies long forgotten. But it must have been buried inside me somewhere, at the bottom of the compost heap, making things grow. In high school and college I wrote articles, essays, poems, reviews. I jotted rhymes on scraps of paper, overheard conversations on bits of napkin. By the time I was grown and working as a journalist—and had finally worked up my nerve to have those wisdom teeth seen to—I was obsessed with found poetry.

Found poetry, like other found art, gets its content from other sources. The writer of a found poem doesn't really write anything. Instead, she looks at the language in something unpoetic—like the owner's manual for an electric stove—and, by rearranging the words or simply taking them out of context, turns it into a poem. (The title of that manual, *Know Your Range,* fairly begs to be turned into a poem, if you ask me.)

Once I started looking for hidden poems, I saw them everywhere: on street signs and television, in SAT prep books, menus, and spam e-mails. It was different from any writing experience I'd had. It felt like that wonderful Emily Dickinson line about writing, only turned inside out. Tell all the truth, but tell it slant, she wrote. Once you started seeing slant, the truth was right in front of you. How could you keep from telling it?

❋

When I finally got to the dentist's office to have my wisdom teeth out, I acted cool, but I was sick with fear. As I followed the nurse down the hall to the surgery room, I actually considered turning on my heel and running, weighing the embarrassment it would cause my mother, who was sitting in the waiting room, when they would grab me under the armpits and pull me back in with my feet dragging along the floor.

I sat back in the chair with three nurses around me in a ring. The doctor slipped a needle beneath the skin on the underside of my elbow. I lifted my face to look up at him for reassurance, but instead my eye snagged on the awful metal instruments lined up on their tray, gleaming at me from under a paper napkin. A cold feeling washed over me, and for the first time in years I tried to pray. Once again, I found I couldn't do it. There was silence on both ends of the line, like a long-standing fight that neither person can remember starting but no one wants to be the first to end. The drug seeped into me, and the contours of the room appeared to buckle and heave nastily before everything went black.

Obviously, I survived—and with a vengeance. My cheeks were distended for a week solid and, for some reason I couldn't bring myself to wonder about, I had a black eye. I was a slave to my painkillers. Every four hours I took another big horse pill that dulled the pain and gave my thinking a lovely, loose quality.

During one of those trippy painkiller afternoons, I was lying on a spot of sunshine on my bed, drowsing like a cat, not really awake but not asleep either. I started thinking about how I couldn't wait to forget all this mess and get back to my poems. There was one in particular that I'd just started piecing together from a 1948 Boy Scout Handbook—just looking at it made me feel warm inside.

The poem was taken from two sections. One was on hand signaling, which is one of many methods of communicating when you are alone and in distress in the wilderness. The other section was about learning your own limitations. A good scout has to know himself well enough to know when he can do things on his own and when he needs to ask for help. The first section was called "Find Your Way," and I'd made that the title of the poem. I picked it up and read it.

With simple means
and using your own personal measurements
determine a height you cannot reach
and a width you cannot walk.
Call loudly for help if you are alone.
Call loudly for help if you are alone, and keep on
calling.

I was thunderstruck. The reason I loved making found poems was because it was different from other writing, where you have to imagine an audience and have no idea if anyone will ever read it anyway. Looking outside myself for poems was like asking the universe a question and actually getting an answer. It was—well, it was like a two-way dialogue.

Oh, that was it! Those poems were my prayers! Making them connected me to the people whose language I borrowed, like those little scouts, grown men now with families, some of them gone. But they connected me to something bigger than that, too. All the time I was listening so hard for the God in my head, God was in the language all around me. And when I lost my own voice, the world around me provided the words. It was a surprise for me to realize, sitting up in my spot of sun, that, even after I thought I had quit, I'd kept on praying and worshiping, loving and being loved back.

I still struggle to understand what I have found in my found poems. I'm not saying I have it all figured out. But I do know this: I was alone, and I called for help. I called loudly, and I kept on calling, and someone answered.

Seventeen

BECOMING THE IMAGINED

Rachel Gaffron

My mother likes to tell the story of how, at age two, I stood beside her as she wrapped Christmas presents making page after page of illegible ball point pen scribbles in a small dime store note-book. She inquired as to what I was doing. I responded by care-fully "reading" her a story from my toddler doodles. I have always been a writer, but between the ages of two and twenty-two my writing self went underground. In a life dictated by church in-volvement, it was more acceptable to participate in *social* groups: concert band, Madrigal choir, thespian clubs, and a graphic de-sign studio. I wanted to write, but I was never allowed any private time. I studied English literature in college because the only op-portunity to be near writing was to read the writing of others.

Ironically, my writing self was reawakened during a year of visual arts study. Finally, I was encouraged to invest hours in quiet observation and work. I would stare at people, trees, reflections on water, sunlight in cornfields, shadows of classrooms. But my first reaction for interpreting what I saw was not to grab for a particular color of paint or thickness of charcoal. Instead, I grasped for a palette of words. What adjective to describe the light on our model's face? What verb to speak of the wind on a lake? I knew I had chosen the wrong course of study when I found myself scribbling stories and poems again, though this time in my art history notebook as I waited for the weekly slide show of great masters to begin.

Now I write, on average, three hours a day. It is the most natural way for me to express myself, to interpret the world around me and to invent new ones. I am learning that creativity emerges from the discipline of action and the intuition of rest. I cannot determine how my work will be interpreted, though I may sit down to create something with specific intention. The difficulty in birthing art is not to let its product overshadow its process. The more I become comfortable with the rhythms of a creative life the more I recognize that all I can be responsible for is doing the work itself. But I continue to struggle with the influence of Protestant culture on my decision to be a creative professional. I feel disillusioned by misunderstandings of the role of artist: as prideful egotist, as lonely prophet, as sinful hedonist, as untouchable genius. Yet, I intuitively know that using my sensory skills to interpret the world I live in is to honor Godde[1] and the gifts that have been blessed to me.

I am inspired by the idea of a culture that honors the body, synthesizes creative expression with religious ritual, and deeply values the wisdom of the earth. What excites me most about being a writer—influenced by a holistic feminism and a compassionate Christianity—is the creative opportunity to imagine this integrated vision for humanity and to craft it on paper. These core values are central to my faith, my feminism, and my chosen art.

✤

I believe art exists in and of itself as a human creation. I prefer a holistic definition of the term art to include the following categories: performing (music, theater, and dance), literary (prose, poetry, and storytelling), handcrafted (textiles, ceramics, jewelry, and bookmaking) and the visual (sculpture, painting, installation, and film). In the last century, these categorical boundaries have been stretched and reshaped in light of new technologies like electronic media; performance movements like Fluxus[2]; and social experiments like the Bauhaus,[3] which proposed the integral relationship between form and function. No matter what its final incarnation, whether it is an ephemeral performance piece or a Miró painting, I believe art is dynamic. Art can wake us up to the world of possibility around us, to the vibrating hum of creation, and to the depth of mystery within our own souls. Art can serve as a conduit between finite viewer, infinite creative force (or Godde), and finite artist. Neither Godde nor the interpretation of stories in the Bible is limited to or trapped within a physical artwork, but I believe divine revelation is always possible in the *presence* of art.

Theological interpretation also has an active quality. Like our understanding of art, we construct theology from others' experiences of Godde as well as our own. Theology is grounded in a tradition but shaped by an ever-evolving human interpretation. My own tradition is rooted in the reformed theology of the United Methodist Church, though I continue to inform my Christianity in a postmodern age that embraces the pluralism of other faiths and their disciplines. I believe in a Godde who is both the holy other and the wellspring of spirit within each of us. I am moved by Paul Tillich's observations that "God is the ground of being" and yet "there is a God beyond God."[4] I am acutely aware of our current brokenness from Godde. God in contemporary America has been relegated to a small-minded square of lawn surrounded by a white picket fence, a domesticated deity that for many endorses an agenda of violence. In my theology, Godde is always larger than the anthropocentric model espoused throughout our Western canon.

Ironically, it is often the art of our great masters that is held up as *the* truth about Godde or the Bible instead of as *a* truth. When art is allowed more power than it deserves and its content is misunderstood or taken out of historic context, then often the work itself is dismissed as false and unnecessary. We should not encourage artists or viewers to limit their imaginative interpretations of our traditional canon. We should always be mindful that our creativity, however talented or flexible, is always too small to seize upon the *entirety* of the Divine.

The *visual* arts are more easily dismissed as passive, decorative paintings when we do not physically know the smell of linseed oil, the stain of red paint under our fingernails, the mysterious process of independent creation. We bodily know the sensation of air pressed through our lungs as we sing "Joy to the World" on a Christmas morning, its trumpeting anthem reverberating in our ears. We know by heart the ritual movements of pew to hymnal to prayer to kiss of peace. We know, too, the rhythm of scripture, liturgy, and Gospel lesson all read and said with the pattern of tongue and teeth and voice. Most of us do not know the active texture of painting and sculpture, especially when our first lesson at an art museum is do not touch. The visual arts offer us opportunities to see deeply, as well as the tactile sensations of smooth paint and bristle-brush and gooey clay most of us haven't known since kindergarten. I think there is a synergy between these two skills, that in order to see we must also engage in the practice of making visual images ourselves. What would happen if instead of being asked to describe verbally our understanding of Godde, we were asked to draw it?

❖

Robin Jensen explores the relationship of artist and congregation in *The Substance of Things Seen: Art, Faith and the Christian Community.*[5] She has two goals in her work with seminary students: first, to reintroduce them to the act of observation, and second, to reawaken an interest in expressing ideas through visual images. Both of these tasks encourage the lay-artist to "begin to understand what the artist sees, and how an artist's imagination plays with the basic material of observation."[6] I agree with her conclusion that we must first recover our somatic knowledge in order to abate fear in the face of personal expression. The arts provide an opportunity to tangibly express our life experiences. As Jensen shrewdly observes, we engage in the work of learning with our whole bodies just as we can understand Godde through the physical form of Jesus. She writes, "the notion that theological insight can come through an artist's creative expression is justified at the very center of our confession of faith."[7]

❈

"Jesus loves me this I know, for the Bible tells me so . . ."

I do not remember "knowing" Jesus' love through reading the Bible, an irony since I drank books like water as a child. Instead it was through music, especially the weekly hymns, during which I knew the presence of Godde's love surrounded us. We United Methodists sang all six verses of every hymn and with an average of four hymns per service, plus the doxology and benediction blessing, we were in for a lot of singing on a Sunday morning. I watched families balance babies on hips as they rose to sing together from the blue hymnal. This bound prayer was held in mismatched pairs of hands as it was shared between husband and wife, sister and brother, friend and cousin. Then we congregants became a spontaneous choir. We were loud and passionate and holy. I heard my honeyed soprano against my neighbor's contralto. I observed my father at his chair by the pulpit and knew the sound of his baritone in my ear. All of our voices swelled in sound, a motion that matched the expanse of air around my own lungs and heart. This physical moment in church informed my intuitive knowledge of the Holy Sprit. The message "Godde is love" was felt in song. I wish there had been similar opportunities with dance and paint and poetry.

The sensory memories of singing in church along with the energy of my creative process and the joy I find in color and nature all connect me with infinite mystery. I do not remember a time in my life when I needed to question the existence of Godde for myself, but I have spent too much energy defending my belief system to others. I was ostracized in public school for being a pastor's kid. I had no answer for a history teacher's questions as to why the Christians reasoned the genocide of native peoples with manifest destiny. I was mocked in my undergraduate courses for "needing a crutch called god." But I was also confused by Sunday school teachers obsessed with burning in hell, parishioners more interested in Jesus' death than his life, and liturgy that clung tightly to masculine symbols of the Divine.

As Robin Jensen explains in chapter 4 of her aforementioned book, the distance that has emerged between artists and the church since the sixteenth century has caused "the church as an institution to lose something crucial: its imagination."[8] We are in need of resuscitating our ability to empathize with the poor and downtrodden in the world. We are in need of rethinking our institutional policies to be more inclusive and tolerant. We are in need of filling ourselves with the Holy Spirit to repair this brokenness. These needs depend on the skill of imagination. So often the responsibility of the artist in the church is to defend the legitimacy of our work to the very people who need its vision the most. The artist is saddled with the responsibility of making his or her work as well as explaining it. Interestingly, the four main problems Jensen describes between the church and the visual arts are also potential sources for renewal and transformation. Art embodies each of these categories: it can be decorative, didactic, an aid to devotion, as well as prophetic.[9] Art, too, is bounded only by our imaginations. But is our contemporary Christian church capable of nurturing artists so they are able to make their work?

❋

I wonder what a parish would have done with a character like Vincent Van Gogh. He, too, was a man living in an era broken by industry and war. He lived off of the charity of his family while he pursued admission to seminary in vain and then began a volatile relationship with paint. Van Gogh's letters to his brother Theo are filled with a passion for ideas, evangelism, and visual invention. But like the postcard reproductions of his infamous sunflowers, we have flattened his life into a legend. Now we only know him with the salacious, sensational details: the unrecognized genius, the poverty, the ear.

I did not understand the power of Van Gogh until I was immersed in his paintings at the Art Institute of Chicago several years ago for a show entitled "Studio in the South: Vincent Van Gogh, Paul Gauguin and the Yellow House." I had become too accustomed to his paintings, even his masterpiece, *The Starry Night*, as decorative tedium on the backs of playing cards, stretched across dorm room walls, t-shirts, umbrellas, and tea trays. It is difficult to see anew when our media-saturated culture instructs us to see a specific way. "Been there, *seen* that" comes to mind. This developed apathy occurs within the liturgy and text of our churches, as well. Can we learn to see beyond the apple, the serpent, the almighty God when viewing our own creation story?

The Starry Night offers something new to us every time we encounter it, but its commodified history threatens the deepening of our relationship with the work. So, too, we are in danger of not seeing Van Gogh's art without it being eclipsed by his celebrity star. The very exercise of "learning to look" at something so familiar is perhaps another way of being able to apply this skill to our active imaginations in the church. Art and theology can be overmarketed to the demise of the work itself, as well as to its participants. Art and theology both exist to expand our understanding of the Divine and our relation with creation. The more we are willing to grow as Christians in our understanding of the complexity of art and theology, the better we are able to exercise our own powerful gifts of imagination.

It has been my experience that church congregations are often just as insensitive to interpreting art as they are to nurturing artists. Artists need space and time in which to create. They need to be trusted instead of feared within their spiritual communities, and most importantly, their creativity needs to be recognized as a holy gift. Deborah Haynes addresses these concerns in her book *Art Lessons: Meditations on the Creative Life*,[10] encouraging that a "theology of art" be developed. She summarizes the artist's role with the following: "a theology of the arts is based on the conviction that the artist has a personal calling, a vocation, to interpret the dilemmas we face, thereby giving voice to hopes and fears, experiences and dreams."[11] An artist is called to interpret and create in a similar way a pastor is called to preach and minister to the world. In order for art and theology to have a relationship, the communal church must mend its understanding of the creative life by recognizing the divine calling of the artist, as well as resisting the temptation to box us into an unimaginative agenda for which to create.

All of us need the arts in order to understand our humanity, as well as to be more human. Art is more than a step-by-step exercise during Sunday school with cotton balls and a glue gun. Art is more than a touchy feely verse of rhyme. Art is underserved and misrepresented when it is *only* understood as an integrative tool for spiritual awakening. Art is expressive, active, and often alarming. Art serves the truth as much as it does beauty. The responsibility of the prophetic artist is to offer creative solutions to the divisive "isms" of our world, to invent, to inspire, and to integrate theory with action. But the church has a responsibility to the artist to be open-minded and imaginative, too. Art and its interpretation help make us critical thinkers and relational beings. How we imagine Godde and spiritual community influences the way we interpret and respond to the moral issues of our time.

And so I return to my notebook to create. *Creativity* has always been one of my favorite words, its five frolicking syllables full of possibility and akin to spontaneous joy. When I am blue with worry, disenchanted by the world's cynicism, the word *creativity*—even whispered to myself—ignites the void with a sparkler's sizzling power: I can write looping tangerine-flamed words into any night's sky. I am certain creativity is an eternal flame we each carry deep within us. We must overcome our fears to embrace creativity's potential as one of our most poignant gifts from Godde. We will become what we are able to imagine.

In Search of Creativity

DISCUSSION QUESTIONS

1. How do you feel creative in your life? What traditional and nontraditional media of creativity do you engage in?
2. What supports your creativity? Where do you turn to be renewed in your creativity? How do you nurture your creativity?
3. What blocks your creativity? What successful ways have you developed to work through these blocks?
4. In what ways does our society support creativity? In what ways does our society suppress creativity?
5. Do you have role models that inspire your creativity? Who are they and how do they inspire you?
6. Is there room for creativity in your faith or spirituality? Have you reimagined any traditional aspects of your faith creatively?
7. Is there room for creativity in your feminism? How has feminism encouraged you to be creative?
8. In what creative ways have you blended your faith and feminism?

ACTION ACTIVITIES

1. List ways in which you are creative, including your talents, gifts, and aspirations. Take one of your visioning ideas from part 1 or part 2 of this book and outline a way to make your vision a reality using your gifts of creativity as well as individual and community talent.
2. Revisit any narrative you have written about your search for a feminist faith, but do not feel constrained by the written word alone. Mix media! Write, sing, dance, paint, or sculpt your story. Share your creation with others.

3. Pinpoint an experience of conflict or an experience of joy having to do with your faith, your feminism, or the intersection of faith and feminism in your life. Use a new artistic medium to stretch yourself and express this experience creatively.

Part Four   **IN SEARCH OF TENSEGRITY**

*Faith. Feminism. Until a few years ago, it seemed
impossible for Rachel to unite these words with an
"and" since they were relegated in her life to the status
of either/or. She could practice her Christianity or she
could be a feminist. How could she be both?*

*Claire struggles with the same paradox in her graduate
religion classes. She opposes the Catholic Church's refusal
to ordain women, and yet she feels most at home in the
rituals of her tradition.*

*We are both learning that to be true to ourselves,
we must simultaneously hold on to the often-competing
ideas surrounding faith and feminism. It takes a great deal
of intention and creativity to find communities that also
support this paradox.*

And so we need a new word for our predicament:
tensegrity. The architect Buckminster Fuller coined this
term to describe the integrity of tension when, ironically,
the competing forces of a structure make it stronger.
Likewise, faith and feminism can be held together in a
strong structure of belief despite their incongruity.
We hope you are able to unite faith and feminism in your
life by honoring integrity, valuing community, practicing
creativity, and embracing the mystery of tensegrity.

Eighteen

THE TENSEGRITOUS EXPERIENCE OF A ROMAN CATHOLIC FEMINIST

Claire Bischoff

hen I was in seventh grade and preparing to help my grandparents celebrate their fiftieth wedding anniversary, I had that "click" moment made famous by second wave feminists, that moment when you realize, for all surface indications to the contrary, patriarchy still rears its ugly head. To mark this major marital milestone, my grandparents planned to have a special mass at their home church, which was less than a mile down the road from my family's home parish. At the time, our parish had the practice of training youth to be altar servers when they were in fifth grade. Since my parents always stressed the importance of serving our community, and because it beat bearing the frigid Minnesota mornings as a crossing guard, my younger sister and I both became altar servers as soon as we were old enough. To be truthful, I actually enjoyed this opportunity to be more intimately involved in the mass. Not only was I drawn in by the rhythm of the liturgy, but also sitting on the altar in front of the entire congregation kept me alert and engaged in a way that sitting in the pews did not.

For the anniversary mass, my grandparents tried to involve as many family members as possible, and they thought that it would be wonderful for my younger sister and me to be the altar servers. However, since the pope had not yet officially approved the Roman Catholic Church's use of female altar servers, and since my grandparents' parish was more conservative than our own, the pastor told my grandparents that their granddaughters simply could not participate in the celebration in this way.

Hurt and confused, I tried to make sense of the situation. At my home church, with almost three years of experience to my name, I was one of the senior altar servers and more than capable of assisting at an anniversary mass in front of my grandparents' family and friends. What was appalling and almost incomprehensible to me was that it was not my ability that was the problem; it was my gender. I could not give my grandparents the gift of assisting at their anniversary mass solely because I was a girl. Besides instilling in me the value of service, my parents never gave me any reason to think that girls were somehow inferior to boys. They were strict believers that their children, both daughters and sons, could do whatever they set their minds to do. To this day, I remember my grandparents' church as a darker, colder place than my home church. Part of this may be due to architectural variation, but my memory has been shaded primarily by sitting in the pew and watching as two boys no one in our family knew served my grandparents' anniversary mass. Thus began my tensegritous relationship with the Catholic Church, a church I would never be able to accept uncritically again.

In the years that followed, I often asked why women could not serve as priests and deacons in the Catholic Church, but parish priests and high school religion teachers never could provide me with satisfying answers. In college, when my dismal experience with organic chemistry convinced me that medicine was not my calling, I floundered for a semester, trying to find a satisfying direction for my study. Through a January term theology class, which I registered for simply to get the credit out of the way (and to spend more time with my boyfriend, who was also enrolled), I rediscovered my passion for the academic study of religion, dormant since some wonderful religion classes in high school. After declaring a religion major, and tired of not having the answers I was searching for, I spent an entire semester studying the issue of women's ordination in the Catholic Church. What was oddly encouraging coming out of those months of study was my discovery that thought had been put into the church's position on the ordination of women; it was not completely arbitrary. Even if I could not agree with the conclusion that the church had reached, at least I knew the logic behind its position and could argue more intelligibly against it.

❈

As a seventh grader, I felt deeply hurt by the Catholic Church, and like many emotional wounds, it has never completely healed. It is a hurt that I continue to struggle with, which at times is more difficult to assuage than at others. When I first encountered feminist theology in college, this hurt was at its most excruciating. In a way I could not have understood as a seventh grader, my eyes were opened to the strong patriarchalism in the Roman Catholic tradition. When I attended mass with family over Thanksgiving break that year, I almost had to remove myself from the assembly. Not able to concentrate on worshipping, all I could do was fixate on the signs of patriarchy and misogyny that were now so readily apparent to me. I was so filled with rage that weekend that I began to contemplate leaving Catholicism and potentially Christianity altogether.

Luckily, before I made such a drastic move, I received much needed advice from one of my professors. I will always remember the wisdom he offered us when one of my classmates asked, "What do you tell people who ask you about switching denomi-nations or religions?"

"No one grows up in a particular denomination or religion by accident," he explained to us. "If you can no longer find God where you are at, then it is time to move. If you still encounter God in your tradition, then stick around and work to change what you find less than loving and life giving."

The more I thought about this advice, the more sense it made. As a corollary, I have not moved to Canada even though I do not agree with every law on the books in the United States. Because there is much about my country that I value, I stay, I vote, and I get involved to try to change things for the better. At this point in my life, I have taken a similar stance toward Catholicism. I stay because there are aspects of Roman Catholi-cism that I could not root out of myself if I tried and parts that I cherish deeply because of the contribution they have made to my life. I stay because I hope that my dissenting voice can make a difference.

This staying has required mental agility on my part. While it sounds as if I have found peace with being Catholic, I know that the relative tranquility I feel now is not a sign of a permanent armistice. There are still days when I wonder if I am crazy, as a woman, to declare allegiance to an institution that continues to be blatantly patriarchal in many ways. Because I am a feminist, I continue to be bothered by teachings in Catholicism that treat women as anything less than full human beings made in the image of God. The only way I can live with integrity is to hold my Catholicism and feminism in tensegrity. This means that I both defend Catholicism against people who feel that it is too flawed to be a viable religious option in our modern world, and also chal-lenge it to live up to its vision of the dignity of all people.

✿

I do not want to give the impression that all of my religious experience as a Roman Catholic woman has been negative. Like many women, my experience with religion has been a strange mix of joy and sorrow, of opportunities for growth and times when my dignity has been denied. What I have discovered in retrospect is that the ebb and flow of my religious experience has helped me to grow as an individual. One trait that grew directly from my experience as a seventh grader was that I developed new eyes through which to view the church and the world. Since I felt that the church's stance on female altar servers was ridiculous, I gained the freedom to analyze critically other church teachings. Since I believed the church was wrong on this issue, I began to discern that powerful institutions were not always right, and this helped me to begin to assess judiciously other institutions in our culture. It is likely that I would have developed critical thinking skills even if I had been allowed to be an altar server at my grandparents' anniversary mass. However, looking back on the experience, I can see that it disposed me to approach power structures, institutions, and supporters of the status quo with a robust hermeneutic of suspicion, a critical frame of mind that is still central to my thought and for which I am thankful.

While this may sound contradictory at first, another constructive aspect of that early experience was that I found myself in a space at the margins of the Catholic community. Originally, I was frustrated by this space. While I continued to participate in the community, I felt as if my critical gaze pushed me to the periphery. Unsure of whom I could trust with this new vision, I felt like an isolated stranger in a once familiar land. My ambivalence left me tired; I longed for the days when I had been able to embrace my faith tradition wholeheartedly and without reservations. As my thoughts matured, however, I discovered that this marginal space, while at times difficult to inhabit, is also a space of creativity. It is a place from which I am free to reframe and reimagine parts of the tradition so that they are more nurturing for women's spirituality. While I have never been as marginalized as some members of our church or our society, I further believe that my experience at the margins has helped me to develop a deep-seated compassion toward others who find themselves as less than full participants in the church and in society.

❋

My early encounter with the way gender shapes religious experience has led me to seek out further studies about women and religion. In both my undergraduate and seminary work, I have tended to gravitate toward any class that has "women" in the title. In my first semester of seminary, this interest led me to register for an online class offered through another institution entitled "Women in the History of American Religion." Obviously, not every student shared my enthusiasm because the class was cancelled due to a lack of registration.

Being intensely interested in the subject, I e-mailed the professor, Mary Bednarowski, whom I had never met, and made my case for taking the course as an independent study with her. I have never asked Mary why she agreed to take on an independent study with someone she did not know who was not even attending the school at which she taught, but I would like to think it had something to do with her desire to share the stories of women's struggles to find authentic religious identities with another woman who was thirsting for these narratives. Mary's agreement to do this class with me was one of many instances in which women involved in religious studies or religious communities have gone out of their way to advise me in my academic studies and in my faith struggles. This is one of the most positive things I have experienced as a woman in a religious context—the sense of camaraderie among religious women that is nurturing, challenging, and inspiring.

As a final project for my class with Mary, I worked on unearthing the history of women's involvement at my home parish, which is still my parents' place of worship and my former employer. I dug through boxes of archives from the women's Altar and Rosary Society, which had been meticulously kept by Beverly Barrett, the unofficial historian of the parish. To get a more personal sense of how women have been involved in the life of the parish, I also interviewed a number of women, some of whom had been founding members of the parish in 1936. Because I brought with me my bias of gender having a negative impact on my religious experience, and because I assumed that things were even better today than they were fifty years ago for women in the church, I expected to hear from these women how much things have changed, how much more involved in the life of the church women are now, and how limited women felt in their roles in the church before Vatican II and the feminist movement.

As it turned out, what I expected to hear and what these women actually told me were two different things entirely. In fact, I kept fishing with my questions for one of them to tell me how dissatisfied they had been with the patriarchy of it all, but it was almost as if they did not understand the question; it was so far afield from their experiences. Instead, I repeatedly heard how women had been "the backbone of the church" and the "life-sustaining force in the parish."

When I examined the official published history of my home church, the Altar and Rosary Society was only mentioned in relation to who held what offices in which years. The rest of the short book focused on pastors, associate priests, and building projects envisioned and led by the male religious leaders. But in listening to these women's stories, I heard a different version of our parish's history. These women were the life and soul of the church; they knew this about themselves, and they did not need anyone else to affirm it for them. With their block program, they developed and nurtured the community. With their fund-raising efforts, they raised the money that supported the building developments. With various projects of all shapes and sizes, these women took care of the needs of the people in the parish and in the surrounding community.

While I would have thought that these women would have been less sure of their role in the church than women are today, I now know this is not true. These women knew that the parish would not survive without them, and although their power was a different kind than was held by the pastor, they knew that they had it and they wielded it wisely for the good of the community. With this new understanding of the role of women in the history of my parish, I have come to a new understanding of my own ministry. It is true that women are not allowed to be ordained leaders in the Roman Catholic Church, and that is something that I will continue to pray to see changed. However, this exclusion should not prevent me from recognizing and celebrating the amazing and vital work women do in the church, that I do in the church. That I acknowledge and give thanks for the power women have in faith communities while also longing for women to be represented in the governing body of our church is just one more example of my tensegritous relationship with the Catholic Church.

❁

In my first year of graduate school, I was presented with an opportunity to bring my experience as a seventh grader full circle. For the first time in the history of Luther Seminary, a Lutheran seminary in St. Paul, Minnesota, a Catholic priest was invited to preach at daily chapel. Regularly, the preacher is in charge of the sermon, and students are enlisted to lead the other parts of worship. To mark the occasion, it was decided that a Catholic person would assist the preacher, Father Lee. Since the one Catholic faculty member was out of town, the responsibility fell to me, one of maybe two Catholic students on campus. As I sat in front of the worshipping community dressed in the same robes as Father Lee sitting next to me, my smile was bittersweet. Had I been at a Catholic seminary, I probably never would have been asked to assist the priest in this way; but since I was at a Lutheran school, what mattered was not my gender, but whether I was willing to take the time to develop the worship plan for that day. And unlike the Lutheran students who assist at chapel on the way to becoming pastors in their own right, I most likely will never have the opportunity to be ordained within my own faith community.

It was a morning when I was ardently proud of being Catholic, yet I also mourned that gender still is a deciding factor for how women can participate in Catholic worship. What has changed most since I was in seventh grade is that I now appreciate the ambivalence of my religious experience and my ability to hold in creative tension the stories of joy and sorrow that have marked my life as a Roman Catholic woman. Ultimately, this skill has helped me be able to hold the ambivalences and the paradoxes that are central to Christian faith in my heart in a way that is more comforting than it is unsettling. I can affirm both the dignity and the sinfulness of humanity. I can recognize the humanity and divinity of Jesus Christ. I can stand in the middle ground between the already and the not yet of the new heaven and the new earth, recognizing the grace that is already in the world and working as a cocreator with God to further the City of God on earth.

Nineteen

Alpha Feminists at the Altar

Laurie Brock

So a priest in the area tells me you're an alpha female with a feminist agenda." (Dramatic pause.) "Are you?" he asked. He was the rector of a parish where I was being placed by the diocesan bishop as my first position out of seminary.

Alpha female is not generally a compliment, from my experience. Usually it is a polite way of calling someone a bitch. Combine that with the f-word (feminist) in certain social circles, and you have a woman no one particularly wants to invite to an afternoon garden party, much less to serve as the assistant priest of an old Southern parish in an even older Southern town. Alpha female feminists, so the legend goes down here, cause problems. In this culture, they do things like point out wage disparity in jobs and opportunity disparity in education. Alpha female feminists think and observe, then point out inequality and paradox, and they are vocal about such things.

In the church, they cause bigger problems. Alpha female feminists aren't satisfied with simply serving God in the roles those in power in the church dispense to them. They are satisfied by serving God in the roles and vocations in which God would have them serve, whether that be cooking the church meals, preaching at services, organizing and leading Christian formation opportunities for children and adults alike, or making sure the altar is completely and perfectly ready for the eucharist. Oh, and celebrating the eucharistic mass. They want the path of ordination open to all, as well. They want to serve God and live out their baptismal covenant as laity, deacons, priests, and bishops. They want the church to live into the equality and inclusiveness of which Christ so fervently spoke.

Yes, alpha female feminists cause problems because they ask questions. They, like their male counterparts, strive to live out the essential message of Christ: love one another. No qualifiers, no exclusions, no exceptions, no excuses.

And yes, I am one of *them*, these alpha female feminists.

And yes, we cause problems, if one sees living out the command to love others as yourself within the framework of equality of service to God and the church as a problem. So instead of serving only in the background, alpha female feminists now stand at the altar as *alter Christus,* another Christ. All celebrants of the eucharistic mass represent the person of Christ at the words of institution. Priests are not simply acting out the historical event of a long-ago seder meal; priests are part of rendering the Last Supper sacramentally present within the community. Women speak the words of institution and offer the sacrament of Christ's body and blood with our feminine voices to the people of God. We serve as deacons, priests, and bishops in the Episcopal Church. We celebrate the Holy Eucharist. We preach the gospel of Christ.

I give you a new commandment, that you love one another. Just as I have loved you, you also should love one another.[1]

As a woman, I am painfully aware that many people in this traditionally patriarchal church do not love that way. Christ loved freely and equally, without regard to status, race, ethnicity, or gender. The Christian church often falls far short of that majestically generous love. The Christian church has often loved in degrees, with exceptions and with exclusions. Those who weren't wealthy enough, educated enough, frightened enough, or perhaps male enough were often excluded from the sacraments of the church and the community of faith. The church still seeks to exclude. Race, economic status, and sexual orientation are among some areas of exclusion that still exist today. Gender is still an issue. I pray words in the celebration of the eucharist that would have resulted in excommunication, if not burning at the stake, if uttered by my sisters of centuries ago. Some of my sisters still face similar consequences.

Living my faith within this church, a church of sinners, is punishing at times. I repeat the words of Christ each Sunday: "love the Lord thy God with all thy heart and soul and mind, and love thy neighbor as thyself."[2] I try, but love gets scarred. My love can be scarred with the pain of experiencing a Christian community in the modern world that gives much credence to status, race, ethnicity, sexuality, and gender. When the body of Christ's followers is scarred, movement can be hurtful and painful. The pain of my scars shoots into my soul when I am reminded of how scarce the inclusive, radical love Christ preached and lived can be within the Christian church. The pain of the collective scars of our life experiences can become so hurtful for those who have lived on the margins of the church that our pain becomes anger.

And on some days, I am very angry at what humans have done to God's church, at what humans have done in the name of rationalizing their limited, exclusive love in the face of the words and commandments of Christ. God's community in Christ is one of inclusion, equality, and love, yet I realize because of my gender, because of the very biological organs with which the

Creator God blessed me, I am, with my many sisters-in-God, not fully part of the patriarchal definition of the church. I regularly have my priesthood challenged by those disciples of exclusion. During a grocery trip, a man informed me that the Bible said women shouldn't be preachers. As I stood holding my baked chicken Lean Cuisine, I wondered if he truly thought I would agree with him and renounce my orders in the frozen food section of the grocery store.

I am angry when I hear God used as a male name, when the image of God is reduced exclusively to a bearded, aged white man instead of a limitless, almighty God. While the theology of the Episcopal Church recognizes that God is not wholly male, the reality is that when I began randomly interchanging feminine and masculine pronouns for God and the Holy Spirit during a Sunday sermon, people in my parish responded with phone calls to the rector to complain. I am aware that while we speak theoretically of an inclusive church, reality is much more difficult to attain because reality demands growth and change.

I am angry when I see statistics that show priests who are women are regularly paid less than their male counterparts for the same job and are rarely called to serve as rectors of large parishes. Many clergy who are women serve in parishes only a few years before moving into nonparish service. Opportunities in a faith that was founded on all people being equal before God are certainly not equal before search committees.

But we are here, alpha feminist females at the altar. We pray prayers written by men that scarcely understand, much less voice, the maternal God who gathers us like a hen gathers her chicks. We hear God and him, he, and his as synonyms, leaving the feminine God languishing somewhere in a theological vacuum. We hear people call male priests "father" with no flinching or thought, but often stand dumbfounded when searching for what to call us.

"What do you want to be called?" several parishioners asked me upon my arrival.

"What would you like to call me?" I replied, hoping they would focus on their relationship with me rather than a title.

When we gather, these alpha females at the altar, we share our stories of pain, of anger, and of the patriarchal oppression that looms over us and presents itself with no recoil or shame. Many of us who are assistant priests realize that the parishes we serve would never consider calling a female rector. Many of us have heard excuses in search processes: "We really like you, but we simply aren't ready for a woman rector." At least they are the honest ones. We talk about our experiences in ecumenical situations, where clergy in denominations who do not recognize the holy call of all of God's creation ignore us or exclude us.

We are, after all, only women.

In the image of God . . . male and female, God created them. God blessed them.[3]

I am a woman. I am a priest. And I grow weary of the chemical combustion when those two facts are blended into my singular person.

When my pain-to-anger has wearied me so that even the anger isn't enough to move my feet forward on this path, I go to the altar. I stand at times. Other times I simply sit on the marble steps, where generations of men have stood.

But they are not here now; I am.

With God. She and I talk. Actually, I talk. She listens.

I vent and bitch. I complain about the labels, about being called the f-word when I point out that of the last four clergy firings in my diocese, three have been women. I tell her about how tired I am of parishioners wondering if I'm a lesbian because I am over thirty and unmarried. Why does that matter? I tell her that parishioners behave badly, really badly, with women, and I think they do so because in their lives, they've always heard that no matter what you do, mother will always love you. Except this mother is a priest and not the answer to every need you've ever had in your life. I lament about being considered lesser than the priests who happen to be male, and knowing that I likely will never be called as rector of a cardinal parish simply because my ovaries got in the way.

I know, I hear a voice, not male or female, respond.

The voice of Christ.

The voice of one who knows exclusion and oppression, who knows the sin of the world and the sin of those who profess faith in God.

I know, I hear this voice repeat, then descend upon me with a breath of understanding.

To stand as alter Christus *is not to stand in power; it is to wash the feet of those who serve. It is to eat with the outcasts, with those who are told by their society they are not enough because of who they are. To stand as another Christ is to serve those who need to be served, to meet people where they are, and to hear my commandments, my teachings, my voice.*

Because you are a woman, because of who I created you to be in this place and time, an alpha female at the altar, you have an understanding that many men do not. You know the feelings of shame when people despise you because you are a woman who is ordained, because you followed my call to holy orders. Think of those who experience shame and humiliation because they are not in the class of white male heterosexual property holders in this one nation under God, in this faith gathered in my name, but not always beholden to my teachings. Because you are among the outcasts in the patriarchal church, you can look into the eyes of those who suffer because of their race, their ethnicity, their sexual orientation, their economic position, or whatever category is not enough to some, and meet them in that place of suffering. Think of the strength you have because of the scars you bear. I, too, suffered through shame and humiliation on the margins of society. I lived with these outcasts as one of them and loved them. I preached God's love from these margins. If Christians are not in these fringes of society, they have not understood me or my gospel.

Because you are a woman in this mostly patriarchal church, you give the feminine a voice. The holy feminine is the voice of Mary, the mother of God; Martha; Mary Magdalene; Sarah and Hagar; Rahab; Ruth, Naomi, and Orpah; and Eve. They are an integral part of creation and resurrection. The great stories of faith need the voice of women, and you continue to give them voice. The soft soprano or lusty alto voice of the alter Christus *who says, "Do this in remembrance of me," reminds the church that creation includes male and female. After all, I birthed all of creation. I know something about being a woman.*

Because you are a woman who serves in my name, you serve all. Perhaps you will not be called to serve at the thousand-member churches with million-dollar endowments, but I am equally present in the small parishes in the inner city or in the rural country. They have an important ministry in the world. Like I said, they who serve the least of these serve me.

The voice of God, the voice of Christ, calms my storm so that I can hear the holy voice within me. At the altar, I, as a priest and a woman, realize God is not patriarchal, nor is Jesus, nor is the Holy Spirit. The institutional church built around God, Christ, and Spirit has patriarchal facets at its best and is an icon of maleness at its worst. But more than two thousand years of patriarchy in the church has not managed to silence the feminine, nor has it managed to silence the radical love of Christ in its members who seek to serve all of creation with such love.

As a priest, I am here, with my sisters. We are not going away. We will not be silenced. We will continue to pray, to celebrate mass, and to remind the people of God of their call:

This is my commandment, that you love one another as I have loved you.[4]

We are here, with our voices and our attitudes and our hopes that indeed the church will surge into the holy world of balance and love.

We are here, these alpha females at the altar, calling the Holy Spirit into the bread, the wine, and the church. We are here, giving the body and blood of Christ to the faithful, in all their brokenness, in all our brokenness.

I am here, this alpha female at the altar, because God has called me to serve God's church and God's people, all of them, wherever they may be.

Twenty

Becoming a Feminist Christian: A Korean-Canadian Perspective

HyeRan Kim-Cragg

*C*hoo-Suk, Korean Thanksgiving Day, begins strangely for me this year. I sit in front of my computer with breakfast: a bowl of granola mixed with raspberry yogurt and a steaming cup of fair-trade coffee. Thanks to one of my Korean Women's Bible Study group members, however, I am not without one important thanksgiving food. Along with my granola, I have prepared the package of *Song-Pyun* that my friend Mi-Sun Kim brought to me so I can taste a bit of the abundance of the Korean harvest season.

Song-Pyun is a half-moon-shaped rice cake steamed on a layer of green Korean pine needles. Its sweetness melts on my tongue and reminds me of my homeland, where the fruits of

God's creation overflow and fill the people's hearts with joy and thanksgiving as full as the fullest moon.

"Tonight, I should go out and gaze at the moon from the Canadian sky and make a wish as all Koreans do," I say to myself as I pull my chair up to the computer desk, knowing I should write as much as possible while the kids are away for the morning.

As a part of my morning ritual, I wind up the blue, battery-free, solar energy radio and listen to the CBC (Canadian Broadcasting Centre) program "The Current," which reports a special documentary called "Ten Years after the War in Africa." The story today is from Rwanda, where the impacts of war are relentlessly overwhelming to the physical, psychological, and social well-being of the country's people. There, even the basics, like food, water, and medical supplies, are far from being abundant or overflowing, far from the reality of the South Koreans' abundant thanksgiving harvest.

Though the last piece of green *Song-Pyun* melts in my mouth, I cannot bring myself to swallow. Instead I ask: How can I feel thankful for having a delicious Korean rice cake, and at the same time, feel so ashamed of having a treat while hearing the stories from Rwanda? Life is a paradox, full of contradictions— abundance and poverty, saving life and killing. In Rwanda, as in so many places, people suffer from racial conflicts and genocide, while other people, including myself, dismiss this violence. Of course, there are the usual excuses: "I did not contribute to that genocide; they are not my people; I am too weak and too little to make that situation better."

Can these excuses be justified? If not, what can I do about it? What can we as Christians do about it? What does it mean to become a feminist Christian living out my faith in a world where unjust relationships are everywhere?

❊

I remember in 1989, while still a student in Korea, the breathless moment when I heard the news that a friend from the Student Christian Movement committed suicide as a way to protest against Noh Tae-Woo's military regime. My heart momentarily stopped. I grabbed my ears, thinking that they must be plugged against this news. I could not imagine my friend wrapping himself in a white cotton cloth covered with messages, calling for democracy and peace in the Korean peninsula before jumping from one of the tallest buildings in Seoul.[1]

My colleagues called him "little Jesus" because his daring decision to sacrifice his life was driven by his Christian faith rather than by naïve political conviction. I felt disturbed by such a radical interpretation, by associating suicide with Jesus and the Christian faith. This interpretation still puzzles me because I have always believed that life is a gift from God, a gift that nobody should take from oneself. I still believe in Jesus as the Christ, not because he died but because he was raised from the dead. I wrestled angrily with these theological and Christological questions, as I sobbed for my fellow student's death.

Then I had to admit that his act of suicide was one of the most powerful actions a human being could commit. It tremendously impacted the movement to bring democracy to Korea. I also realized that his suicide was not an arbitrary action but an action following the long tradition in Korean society of recognizing and respecting suicide for a cause as supremely honorable and courageous. It made sense to me why some Buddhist monks—by burning themselves—as well as Confucian scholars—by drinking poisonous medicine—took their lives when Korea was occupied by Japan in 1910. The action of suicide spoke powerfully against the Japanese colonial invasion and inspired other Koreans to fight for freedom and independence.

Can this Korean cultural act of suicide for a cause be, then, holy and sacred, since it is a concrete act of the selfless love for others? Could this, therefore, be regarded as Christian, and even called atonement or sanctification? Can these two entities, dying and living, Korean culture and Christianity, be compatible and coexistent? Is Christian faith also a paradox as life is a paradox?

My witness to his suicide and theological reflections upon this witness opened my eyes to the real world and opened my ears to the true Christian faith. I was opened like the deaf man who hears after Jesus puts his fingers in his ears, spits and touches his tongue, and finally looks to heaven saying, "'*Ephphatha*,' that is, 'Be opened,'" (Mark 7:31–34). From that point on, my eyes could never be blind to the demonstrations in the streets. My ears could never again be plugged to the cries calling for democracy and peaceful unification.[2] It seemed that all of Korean society, especially around the universities and industrial factories in the urban areas, was shaking. It was the beginning of a social earthquake, as shoulder to shoulder people marched through the streets.

I, too, joined a number of demonstrations. During one, the tear gas was shot directly toward me, leaving my light blue t-shirt with a brown burned scar.[3] The gas poured out from the armed police trucks, and I could not breathe. My eyes stung, and my nose dripped. My whole face was hot and itchy. I wanted to cry but could not.

But I saw Jesus there. He was breathing painfully along with me and the shaken and scattered crowd. He was there in the chaotic streets, where white tear gas powder rose from the ground like hot steam, water from the fire hydrant splashed, and flames burned from broken bottles thrown into the police lines. He was with those who were weeping, fighting, and protesting for democracy. And he called me to follow him. In the midst of this chaotic moment, I sang this phrase from the hymn "I Come to the Garden Alone:" *He bids me go; through the voice of woe his voice to me is calling. And he walks with me, and he talks with me, and he tells me I am his own.*[4] Ironically, it was also a quiet moment, like the pause after that earthquake, both chaotic and peaceful.

❖

Fifteen years later, now in Canada, the voice of woe still calls to me from Korea. It is Jesus calling to me, whispering "*Ephphatha, HyeRan!*" as he puts his fingers into my ears, as he spits and touches my tongue so that I can continually be opened to his people, who are crying and struggling for life—even life beyond death.

My life is a paradox, as I am both privileged and marginalized. I am well educated, ordained, married to a Caucasian man and bilingual in Canadian society. I feel fortunate to live in Canada because it is known as one of the most multicultural, multi-ethnic, and democratic countries on the globe. Canada seeks to become a mosaic society instead of a melting pot, where diversity is advocated and cherished.

This, however, does not mean that all ethnic groups are treated equally in Canada. In fact, Canada is still very much a white-male-Anglo-Christian society—just look at who holds the roles of power in Canada's businesses and government. In this current Canadian context, I experience being marginalized as a Korean woman. I can never fully belong to one group, Korean or Canadian, I am far away from my homeland, and I am always removed from the center of the male-European academy.

Yet this paradox of multiple identities can be liberating rather than oppressing. It is liberating because I can hear more clearly why Jesus is calling me as I am opened to those who have paradoxical identities like I do. Then I begin to see these "marginalized" groups as the "majority" in society, and therefore the task of empowering them is the "major" task, not the "marginal" one. I can also see what Jesus meant when he said that the kingdom of God belongs to those who are like little children (Mark 10:14). I start to imagine how exciting it will be when "many who are first will be last, and the last will be first" (Mark 10:31). Christian faith manifests its truth as it is shaped by our particular life experiences and our particular contexts. Christian faith is indeed a paradox as life is a paradox. Just as the colors of the rainbow are revealed through a prism, our paradoxical life becomes clear as it is reflected within the lens of our Christian faith.

Furthermore, I see my faith being in solidarity with those who are different from and more marginalized than me. As I yearn for my homeland, I see myself walking with Native Canadians in their demonstrations to reclaim their land. Just as I experience racism as a Korean citizen entering the United States, I see myself joining in the Arab-Muslims' protest against racial discrimination post–September 11. As I am often overwhelmed as a mother of two young children, I see myself associated with those who are single mothers. I see Jesus here in Canada, too, with all of these marginalized yet majority people. I hear his voice in the midst of Native peoples' drumming, Arab-Muslims' praying, and single mothers' weeping.

✿

What does it mean to become a feminist Christian living out my faith in this context where unjust relationships are so dominant?

For me, becoming a feminist means identifying myself with the marginalized group.[5] It means sharing our common experiences of marginalization with one another and analyzing these experiences from political, social, and cultural perspectives. It means seeking action toward justice in just relationships.[6] For me, becoming a feminist is more than working for women's issues because who we are as women is more than a gender identity. I cannot be a woman without my ethnic, religious, and marital identities. Becoming a feminist is, thus, fundamentally holistic. It requires all kinds of pieces of who we are as women interwoven together in the fabrics of the political, social, economic, and cultural aspects called life. No wonder life is a paradox, full of contradictions and possibilities, sorrows and joys, despairs and hopes.

For me, becoming a Christian is being faithful to the God who created each one of us. Becoming a Christian means celebrating this life even through death, both of which are graciously granted to us. It means living that life out in right relation to one another. For me, becoming a Christian is being faithful to God revealed in a Jesus who is present in the march for democracy and justice. Becoming a Christian means being opened to the voice of Jesus, which calls me to be with the people who are marginalized and struggling for life, and even choosing death so that others may live.

Becoming a feminist and a Christian, though they are distinctive identities, are closely connected realities. Both seek to celebrate life and to live out one's faith in the promotion of just relationships among *all:* women and men, the Third World and the First World, North and South Koreans, human beings and the whole ecological community.

However paradoxical they seem at times, as far as I can see, feminism and Christianity do not contradict one another. Having said that, I also know that I will always wrestle with contradictory feelings as I seek to live out my faith, just as I did fifteen years ago at the tragedy of my friend's suicide, just as I feel trapped between privilege and marginalization as a married Korean-Canadian-Protestant woman, just as I did with my *Song-Pyun* this morning. Just as life is a paradox, so, too, is becoming a feminist Christian.

As I finish this essay, I can see the full moon outside my window. It is gorgeous—so clear yet so mysterious, so bright yet so dark, so plain yet so deep, so finite yet so infinite. I try to focus on the moon alone, yet I also see the universe around it. I see Korea yet I see Canada yet I see the whole world out there. It is time to go out and make my thanksgiving wish.

Twenty-One

The Darker Womb

Elizabeth J. Andrew

*L*ast October I reached an edge of the feminist map. "Here Be Dragons" was scrawled in fine mediaeval script along the margin. Each time I extended a toe into that danger-ous territory, the women around me flipped. For months I thought I was crazy, too, until I realized there was a pen in my hand and "Here Be Dragons" was really an invitation for me to keep mapping new territory. I'd much rather follow someone else's (that is, some strong, wiser woman's) footsteps. Isn't that the benefit of being in feminism's third wave? I despise smashing solo through untrodden wilderness.

I was on a weeklong silent retreat on the north shore of Lake Superior. This in itself was nothing new; for six years I'd taken this annual retreat, accompanied by three older women I deeply ad-mire. My spiritual director, a white-haired, patchwork-jacketed woman with firm feminist footings, hosted these retreats in her home. Statues of fat goddesses abounded, and yet our focus was thoroughly Christian—time spent apart (just as Jesus did, withdrawing from the crowd) to listen for the spirit's work in and through our lives. Incarnation was the order of the day. Once, during my daily check-in with my director, she cupped a small oval mirror in her palm, naming it a window onto God. When my own reflection filled the glass, I knew how thoroughly God inhabits personhood, Jesus' as well as mine. We began and ended each day with the ringing of the Tibetan prayer bowl and a half-hour of group silence, often focused on a passage from Mary Oliver— "You do not have to be good. . . . You only have to let the soft animal of your body love what it loves"[1]—or Annie Dillard—"Every day is a god, each day is a god, and holiness holds forth in time."[2]

For six years, this retreat was my version of heaven. I sank into the silence, into the depths of breath and being. At night I dreamt of a house-sized crow rising from Superior's surface. During the day I scrambled the rocks along Lady Superior and found an outcropping that resembled a large-breasted woman, legs spread into the water as though awaiting a baby's arrival. I practiced heeding the strange inner workings of the spirit, listening to this presence that had always been with me, even during depressions, even through my rebellions, even when I doubted God's very existence—an accompaniment like the drone of a trustworthy bass note beneath the song of my life. For one week each year, I gave it complete attention. I thought this accompaniment was normal. I never noticed it was there until it was gone.

And last October it was gone. My director rang the bell to begin our grand silence; the brass resounded until its lingering tones were swallowed by quiet and I was left with . . . emptiness. Except for the candles on our altar, the house was dark. Out the windows, Lake Superior was dark. Darkness wrapped a stranglehold around my lungs. I faced seven elongated days of nothingness.

I should have expected it. In the year prior I'd grown suspicious that something was terribly wrong in my spiritual life. Spirit inhabited my lazy cat, the greening lawn, every intake and release of breath, and the more I knew this to be true, the more remote God seemed. All my trustworthy methods of relating to God (meditation, a half-hour swim, church) were falling flat. God, I knew, infused Godself into all creation, yet the *felt experience* of this knowledge was receding as swiftly as my theism. At home, my daily life was jammed with writing and teaching and a girlfriend and a movie theater two blocks away—enough distractions that I never had to sit with emptiness for long.

Here on Lake Superior, with a week of silence looming before me, I could not escape it. During my daily check-in with my director, I bemoaned my forsaken state. "But God is still present!" she protested. A logy, fat summer fly buzzed half-heartedly against the windowpane. "In Africa," she told me, "they don't brush the flies away from children's faces because they believe flies are spirit messengers." I wanted a swatter. Of course God was everywhere, in and through creation. Why could I no longer *feel* it? My frustrated director had no idea. We banged our heads against an invisible brick wall for an hour, and then I returned to my dark room. Prayer was like breathing without the satisfaction of oxygen; I didn't know how essential it had been, how pleasurable, how mundane, until it was gone. Either something was terribly wrong with me (years ago I might have blamed my sinful nature for the rift between me and God, but I'd since become a believer in original blessing.[3] Besides, I was making my very best effort. What more could God ask?) or God had abandoned me. Despite the "God is Love" of my liberal Christian upbringing, despite feminists' assurances that redemptive suffering is bunk, and God would never *will* our pain, God had abandoned me. I was certain of it.

In desperation, I opened the pages of St. John of the Cross. Catholics use the term "consolation" to describe the experiential

presence of God—the feelings, the comforting dreams, the syn-
chronicities that signify the Holy One's activity in our lives. John
described the dark night of the senses, a stage in spiritual growth
when God removes our consolations. It's as though up until now
we've been sucking at God's breast, John writes, and God deter-
mines to wean us. My spiritual state had a diagnosis; I was in the
dark night of the senses! What a relief to have another (albeit a
sixteenth-century Spanish Carmelite priest) describe what I was
going through. Non-Christian feminists ask with incredulity
why I stay inside such a patriarchal faith, and here is why: the
Christian tradition is a map for my experience. Sometimes I must
leave the pew and search musty, antiquated texts to find it, but it's
there. If both the Christians and the feminists had failed me at
this point, I'd be fighting dragons on two fronts. I doubt I would
have survived.

Nothing had prepared me for the wrenching sensation of
God's withdrawal. In fact, I'd been led to believe such an event
was impossible. God would never harm us; God would never pull
away. John acknowledged my feelings of abandonment and still
had words of assurance: "Those of you who find yourselves in this
predicament need to comfort yourselves. Patiently persevere and
do not let yourselves get upset. Trust in God, who does not abandon those who seek him with a simple and righteous heart."[4] The
sensation of God's absence was in fact a restructuring of our relationship. By removing the consolations, God was inviting me to
see God as God is, and not as God benefits me. So much for the
comforting mother sculptures. So much for the assurance of
houseflies, or gentle retreat companions, or my beloved spiritual
director. One face of God is emptiness, and emptiness was now—
is now, because nothing has changed—turned toward me.

All through that week of imploding silence, I leaned on my
new companion in suffering. "The deep suffering of the soul in
the night of sense," John wrote, "comes not so much from the
aridity she must endure but from this growing suspicion that she

has lost her way. . . . She thinks that if she is making a conscious effort . . . and still feels nothing, then she must be accomplishing nothing."[5] After every silent meditation, I wept with frustration because of the terrifying emptiness I met there. I felt nothing; I was accomplishing nothing. "This is no time for discursive meditation," John assured me. "Instead, the soul must surrender into peace and quietude, even if she is convinced she is doing nothing and wasting time."[6] I was far from peaceful about doing nothing. And yet fighting the nothingness was going nowhere; surrender, as unpleasant and antithetical to my feminist leanings as it seemed, at least provided me with direction.

So God was weaning me. Despite John of the Cross's nursing image, the experience of God's separation harkened me back to that bearded man in the sky, God above and we, groveling humanity, down below. I felt jerked around by that master puppeteer. For the ten years I'd been intentional about fostering my spiritual life, I had heeded my creative, justice-seeking, life-affirming impulses by taking enormous risks (leaving a safe public school teaching career for self-employment, publishing a book in which I came out bisexual, overcoming my self-defeating inclinations in order to enter an intimate, committed relationship), and had fed on a steady stream of divine encouragement. Growth in my spiritual life meant progress toward my truest self, and, despite the risks and growing pains, there was always that blessed assurance and divine sustenance. Now, for no reason I could recognize, God had slammed the door, as John so accurately described it. One Jewish Midrash tells of God creating the world, and then deliberately withdrawing from it. *How else might God be in relationship with creation?* the rabbis ask. I pictured the dark void between Godself and our blue-green planet and threw a temper tantrum. Thirty-three years in the faith had taught me God's unfathomable closeness. And now I was taunted by absence.

God "denudes the faculties, the affections, and the senses," John confirmed. "He leaves the understanding dark, the will dried up, the memory vacuous, and the affections tormented by bitter-ness and anguish."[7] *What would the feminists make of this?* I won-dered from my cozy but tormented retreat room. God "takes away from the soul the feelings of pleasure she used to enjoy from spiri-tual blessings. This deprivation is one of the principal requirements for the union of love."[8] Both John's and my experience presented this deprivation as fact, and yet I fought it; it was an unacceptable interpretation; it made God out to be manipulative and controlling. My whole journey of growth as a woman—the whole thrust of the feminist movement—is toward fully owning our strength, our will, and our goodness. Our divinity even, God manifest in our bones and our ability to give birth. We rejoice in our power and in God's invitation to mutual, loving relationship. The idea of surrender, es-pecially to a God who exacts deprivation as a requirement for union, is highly suspect. No one is our master.

And yet John, the lone soul who comprehended my anguish, called upon me to make God my master. The more I read, how-ever, the more complex John's master-God became. Since that re-treat, I've read innumerable texts on the dark night of the soul, and St. John of the Cross is the least patriarchal and most sur-prising among them. His guiding metaphor, which subsequent commentaries often overlook, is the soul as lover, slipping from a still house at night to rendezvous with God. The "master" he refers to is "no other guide / than the one burning in my heart," a light that leads the way "more clearly than the risen sun"—a di-vinity manifest within and through John's being.[9] John's is an erotic love, in the tradition of the Song of Songs and certainly in keeping with Carter Heyward's theology of radical mutuality:[10]

Upon my blossoming breast
Which I cultivated just for him,
He drifted into sleep,
And while I caressed him,
A cedar breeze touched the air.[11]

God rests God's head on John's chest in a divine intimacy I can hardly fathom. The poem ends in orgasmic oblivion, senses suspended and self lost in full, unhindered union.

Here was an image I could sink my heart into. My own intimate relationship was two years old; our honeymoon stage had been swiftly obscured by a growing awareness that my girlfriend was a survivor of early childhood sexual abuse, and at the time of my retreat we were mucking through the worst of it, avoiding physical intimacy for fear of triggering memories, still living separately, rarely able to do more together than cry and read aloud adolescent science fiction. Where John differs from feminists in his portrayal of God as lover is in his utter lack of idealism. Love hurts. His beloved wounds him. "The night is so dark and the way so difficult to speak of," he wails.[12] Humans balk at the annihilation of self that true intimacy entails, John acknowledges; we grieve the loss of our inadequate concepts of God and our self-serving motivations. But these are necessary if we are to love God for who God is rather than for the good feelings God gives us—to love the "God of consolations rather than the consolations of God," as Teresa of Avila put it.[13] My deprivation was real, unasked for, and an invitation to a new depth of relationship. I was beginning to face this challenge with Emily. Did I love her just for her physical affection, just because she made me laugh, just because she was pleasurable to be around? Or was my love one that encompassed her woundedness and our times of separation? All I knew of God up until this miserable retreat was how God affected *me*. What if I left self behind, and sought the great I AM? So God spoke to Job from the whirlwind: "Where were you when I laid the foundation of the earth? Tell me, if you have understanding" (Job 38:4).

Throughout that abandoned week, I forsook my fruitless meditation, laced up my hiking boots, and tromped down to Superior's edge. The waves were thunderous, ocean-sized, smashing. I might not be able to pray, but I could let water's heave and roar wash away my being. A woman's spiritual journey travels through brokenness toward healing, through inadequacy toward our fundamental divinity. But at some point, the balance tips. Our ego is strong enough, our footing firm enough that something dreadful happens. In order to grow further, we must stop adding and begin subtracting. We need to take the self we've spent decades strengthening and trust it enough to let it go. The challenge we feminists face is letting love be our master. "Until the soul surrenders her personal will," John of the Cross wrote, "and goes out into the dark night in search of God, she will not find him."[14] I perched on the rocky shore, my mind erased by the waves' blast, and I took in that huge, watery expanse as best I could. At the edge of all maps there is still more, something greater than personal power, vaster than the mind's capacity, throbbing in our blood's pulse and in the violence of waves. Neither understanding nor will can take us there. Our only way is exquisite risk.[15]

Twenty-Two

Conflicts That Fortify: The Landscape of My Spiritual Home

Kathleen Holbrook

*T*hroughout my childhood, the Stewart Ranch represented a confluence of my deepest fears with the structures that provided rich security. Here my mother and I summered in the acceptance and wisdom of my grandparents' care. I experienced the brightness of the Uintah Mountain meadows with their carpets of wildflowers. I learned the nature of small rivers while on horseback, my arms tight around my grandmother's waist. Grandpa taught me to ride one of our gentle palominos on my own and introduced me to the thrilling taste experience of a salt lick. In the small Church of Jesus Christ of Latter-Day Saints (LDS) chapel down the road, Grandpa performed my baby blessing by which I was given a name. Nature, family, and church welcomed me there and shaped my identity. But there was a darker side to the Stewart Ranch. When I was outside alone, my fears were legion. Vicious animals, vengeful ghosts, and kidnappers (who I imagined followed me wherever I went and do so from time to time even now, when I have my own babies to protect) bided their time in every place that was lush. I believed that some of them sought my body; others prized my soul.

One early ranch morning during the summer of my fourth year, when the sun had just begun to lighten the sky through the eyelet curtains in my mother's room, I heard pain in my grandfather's voice as he called my name. Climbing out of bed, I saw him stretched on the floor across the threshold of his bedroom door.

"I need you to go and get your Aunt Nora," he said.

Grandpa's health had been worsening through the past months—he would be buried in a Salt Lake City cemetery the following Valentine's Day—and he had lain awake in distress that night, waiting for enough daylight so that he could rouse me and send me to his sister for help. Since my mother and grandmother had spent the night in Salt Lake to accommodate their schedule as volunteer tour guides at the Beehive House, a former residence of the Mormon prophet Brigham Young, I was the only one who could go for help. Aunt Nora's house lay the distance of a short city block from ours.

There are more shadows than images in my memory of that morning, sitting in Aunt Nora's kitchen as other family members were dispatched to carry Grandpa into a car and drive him to the hospital. But I recall with clarity the journey to her house, the terror that drove my straining limbs as I ran—how I ran!—accompanied by birdsong, the rustle of woodchucks in the underbrush, and the heady scent of dew on aspen and woodland grass. I hoped the power of our wood's benevolent spirits—the flowers, deer, and other gentle creatures—was sufficient to protect me from the malevolent forces hiding just beyond my vision. And I prayed. I prayed as my mother and teachers at church had taught me—to a loving and powerful Father in Heaven.[1] My fear notwithstanding, I prayed with perfect confidence in God's goodness. I knew that God listened to me. At the age of four, my feelings toward God, informed by Mormon doctrine, were not so different than they are now. I experience him and his mysterious female partner as a haven, as the embodiment of acceptance, as beings who know me and answer my prayers. I credit church teachings for my satisfying relationship with deity.

Just as the context of the Stewart Ranch rouses contradictory emotional states, my experience in the institutional church is not without paradox. My relationship with the LDS Church is strengthened over time by both the glorious and the negative. As in my marriage, in the institutional context of my church, I must exercise patience, must extend to another the grace that I need to have extended to me. This faith-imbued process of forgiving and receiving forgiveness, of remaining committed to a relationship with an imperfect partner—all the while learning to recognize my own imperfections—works little by little to improve both me and that holy other, whether it be spouse or church.

My paradoxical experience with the LDS Church was revealed in stark relief when I entered the LDS Missionary Training Center (MTC), a month after my twenty-first birthday. This collection of flat-roofed buildings, made of sandstone-colored brick with small windows and no architectural details to recommend them, sits on the outer perimeter of the Brigham Young University (BYU) campus, facing the mouth of the small but majestic Rock Canyon two blocks away. Hundreds, if not thousands, of new missionaries are welcomed to the MTC every Wednesday. For some, the buildings signify a religious prison, a penitential monastery from which they cannot wait to escape. For me, this drab complex represented an intoxicating freedom: I would not have to worry about car repairs, budgets, relationships, schoolwork, or the vagaries of dating for my eighteen-month tenure as a missionary.

For the nine weeks I would be at the MTC, I only had to study and contemplate the crags of my beloved Rock Canyon.

Excepting semiannual phone calls home on Christmas and Mother's Day and weekly letters to family and friends, I would have no contact with my loved ones for eighteen months. I would spend two months studying LDS doctrine and the Russian language at the MTC, then move to Russia for the remaining sixteen months of my tenure as a missionary. I would arise each day at 6:00 A.M., retire by 10:30 P.M., and never leave the side of my assigned "companion." While companions were changed every several months, the rule was constant. I would never flirt or be alone in a room with a member of the opposite sex, and, as much as I could, I was to communicate with my colleagues only in Russian. I was told, and I believed, that obedience was the key to my success as a missionary. If I worked hard, followed the rules, prayed, and read my scriptures, I would be happy, and I would accomplish what the Lord wanted me to do as a missionary.

My time in the MTC was predominantly marked by happiness and peace. I loved the eight other missionaries with whom I attended class each day, my teachers were exceptional, and I was possessed of boundless energy and good cheer—the result, I think, of focusing so intensely on learning and doing God's will. My heartfelt testimony, in Mormon parlance, that Mormonism was God's creation also increased during my stay. One of the first days of class, I was in a group of three missionaries, role-playing the delivery of the curriculum we would present during our initial encounter with people who were interested in the church. I described to a fellow missionary, in his role as church "investigator," the story of Joseph Smith, Mormonism's founder. In 1820, Joseph was fourteen years old and confused about the state of his soul, aloof as he was from the sectarian churches of western New York. He read in James 1:5, "If any of you lack wisdom, let him ask of God, that giveth to all men liberally, and upbraideth not."[2] Joseph believed this scripture and went to the woods near his house to pray. At first he was nearly overcome by a dark power, but then God and Jesus appeared, banishing the evil presence and starting Joseph on his prophetic course.

As I described these events, I remembered the terror I had felt at the age of four in my own woods as I ran and prayed. I recalled my faith in God's willingness to listen and to answer. Though only a role-play, my recital of Joseph's story suffused me with feelings of security, clarity, and purity. I had been taught that such feelings indicated the presence of the Holy Ghost, the sacred visitor to discussions that were true and of divine importance. The intensity of these feelings while discussing Joseph's experience strengthened my belief that he did indeed receive instruction from God and that my church was founded on revelation. I experienced varying degrees of this sensation throughout my missionary service and have continued to do so sporadically ever since: while listening to a perceptive comment in church, while helping someone in need, and while holding my baby girls, enjoying their warmth and the scent of their milky breath.

Yet despite the serenity and joy I experienced, the MTC was not without its contradictions and struggles. A few days after my arrival, I was called to act as the Sisters' Leader for the approximately thirty women with whom I worshipped during Sunday services. I was assigned to worship with the International Branch, meaning the other hundred or so people in this improvised congregation spoke little or no English. I was to check in with the female members of this branch at the end of each day to make sure they were getting along well—and obeying the rules. Each Sunday, I was to attend a meeting with all of the male leaders in the branch and the members of our "branch presidency," three middle-aged men who lived in the area and had been called to oversee the operations of our group. Although the nineteen-year-old male leaders were technically responsible for female missionaries ("sisters") as well as male missionaries ("elders"), the strict limits on male-female relationships required that I serve as a leader, since I could speak freely with the sisters and visit them in their residences.

Thus on my first Sunday in the MTC, I left my companion to wait with two other sisters in the sterility of the hall's cinderblock walls and industrial carpets while I attended the leaders' meeting. I sat in a small, crowded room filled with men, the smell of hair gels and shaving creams mingling with the wool of their bargain suits. While the branch president was probably in his fifties, the elders in the room were younger than I, most of them barely nineteen. After an opening prayer, the president turned to me and asked several pointed questions about how the sisters were doing. I answered the best I could, remarking on a few cases of illness and the generally high morale that I had observed. Following my report, the president surprised me by asking me to leave. The elders in the room each had responsibility for small groups of missionaries, called districts, while I was responsible for all of the women in the branch. Yet I had to report and leave this meeting before any of the nineteen-year-old elders in the room even spoke, as if my hearing their words would have been a security breach. My cheeks bore humiliation's first flush as I gathered my things and made my way out the door. I resolved to ask my branch president about the reason for my expulsion, hoping that my question would either show him that I should stay for the entire meeting or allow him to explain the protocol in a way that would help me to feel more peaceful about it.

Sisters and elders were required to send a weekly letter to the branch president, so I described my concern in that week's letter, explaining that I had felt uncomfortable at being asked to leave in such an abrupt manner. I asked that he provide me some insight about why things were done as they were. I received no response. But the next week at our meeting, after the opening prayer, instead of hearing my report, the branch president excoriated me in front of the elders, telling me repeatedly that women in the church do not hold leadership positions, then asked me to leave and to speak with one of his counselors—his assistant in the branch presidency.[3]

The counselor with whom I spoke had a different agenda for me than our president. He was a BYU professor and—without criticizing the president—seemed mostly intent on assessing how much damage had been done and making veiled suggestions that sexism in the church would die out eventually. Our president was not from North America, and I suspect his caustic approach to my concerns was heavily influenced by his cultural background, leading him to exploit the negative potential of Mormonism's patriarchal system.[4] Still, despite the calming influence of the thoughtful counselor, I found it difficult to forget the episode. This memory affected the rest of my stay in the MTC. Whenever a speaker directed his talk toward the elders instead of the missionaries, saying things like, "It's great to have a chance to share my thoughts with you elders this evening" or "Elders, turn to your companion and ask him . . ." I felt once more the slap of the president's confrontation.

Bearing these wounds, I entered the "mission field" of Russia thousands of miles down the Volga River, where I witnessed misogyny completely different than what I had experienced in the MTC. Whereas my frustrations at the mouth of Rock Canyon resulted from women's contributions being limited and ignored, in Russia I met women who worked long days, then came home to fix dinner, wash the laundry by hand, do the dishes and other household chores, and tend to the children, all without help from their husbands. All too often, husbands were out drinking and looking after mistresses while their wives struggled through these exhausting routines. When a handful of these men joined the church, their religious responsibilities impelled them to stop drinking away the family's meager income, forsake other women, and play an active role in the rearing of their children. Ironically, despite the patriarchal system of Mormonism, the LDS emphasis on male responsibility and leadership made men into more attentive partners and fathers and improved the lives of their wives and children. When men live according to the teachings of the LDS Church, they do not belittle, betray, or neglect their loved ones. Instead, they express love, spend time with their children, and pray with and for their wives.

As a missionary, I watched families blossom as men began to take on their share of interest in and responsibility for their families. On the other hand, I listened as my twenty-nine-year-old Armenian companion from Moscow complained because we had to get permission from a twenty-year-old boy in order to travel outside of our work area. I understood her frustration. All missionaries had to get permission to travel outside of their areas, but the individual in the position to grant permission would always be male, never female. Yet the irritation of this unequal representation was less significant than the joy I felt when I saw the increased happiness, hope, and peace of people whose perspectives and beliefs led them to join the church. In my mind, the positive ramifications of church teachings were more significant than the negative impact of a patriarchal system. The consequences of patriarchy rankled, but ultimately they did not jeopardize my allegiance.

Successive challenges followed by renewed commitment have strengthened my bond to the church much like a friendship that survives a period of conflict grows increasingly intimate and resilient. Furthermore, this process has resulted in my obtaining a richer understanding of the church, a relationship less limited by superficial assessments and oversimplifications. Active engagement with Mormonism allows me to witness the benefits of LDS teachings, both for my own soul and for the increased happiness of others.

As my life progresses, I continue to experience moments when the influence of the LDS Church has surprised me in its ability to promote feminist priorities. As I witnessed in Russia and continue to perceive here in the United States, one of the key conditions that prevents women from realizing their full potential as participants in the world is a lack of time caused by disproportionate responsibilities in the home. In *Overworked American,* Juliet Schor found that women with families work an average of eighty hours a week when time spent on child care, housekeeping, and work outside the home was tallied.[5] LDS teachings promote the flourishing of women through their emphasis on women's and men's shared responsibility for child rearing and household work.

Recently, I had to rethink some of my assumptions about patterns of female empowerment among my colleagues versus those in the LDS Church. As head teaching fellow for a popular religion course at Harvard University, I arranged for weekly teaching staff lunches. One week, when a prominent guest was scheduled to lunch with us before addressing our class, we decided to have our meal brought to us rather than going to a restaurant. When we finished eating and the time came to clear away the lunch dishes and walk to class, seven female teaching fellows immediately got to work clearing things away. The two male teaching fellows moved to a couch to get advice from the male guest (strangely, this was the most attentive either of them was to any of our guest speakers all semester), while the male professor found a chair and finished preparing his opening remarks for class. All four of these men prided themselves on their social progressivism, including sensitivity to feminist concerns. The women were also feminists, two eschewing makeup and wearing androgynous hairstyles and clothing so they would be treated as individuals rather than as women. In this group of feminists, in a situation that called for shared responsibility, the women in the group stepped up to do the traditional "women's work" that needed doing and did not question the men's noninvolvement, and none of the men offered to do their share.

As I helped to clear away our lunch, I remembered a scene from the previous year. My cousin, who is decidedly not socially or politically progressive, and his wife had invited several family members to their home for dinner. Throughout the meal, my cousin and his wife took turns tending to their newborn son. After dinner, while the baby nursed, my cousin cleared the table, did all of the dishes, and even wiped off all of the countertops, including the placemats we had used. Male LDS church leaders taught him that he should be an active participant in the rearing of his children and the running of his household, and he was. While my progressively leaning colleagues did not act on their feminist beliefs on this occasion, my cousin, although he associates with a patriarchal religion and would probably never call himself a feminist, lives out his marriage commitment in a feminist way if shared responsibility is used as the benchmark.

These are anecdotes; I'm certain it would be easy to find counterexamples of progressive men who act consistently on their feminist beliefs and Mormon men who do not live up to the LDS expectation of shared responsibility in the home. Yet these examples illustrate truths that heavily inform my loyalty to the LDS Church. While some aspects of the patriarchal system do not accord with my understanding of what is best for women, some church teachings can improve women's lot. In the end, however, my devotion to the church is not solely about what it does for women in general or for me personally as a woman. My core devotion to the church centers on the way its teachings shape and enhance my relationship with God. I do not expect perfection because I realize that my understanding of God is mediated by human frailty, both my own and that of those with whom I worship. I have never felt justified in directing my frustrations about human error toward deity. I believe the LDS teaching that we are all sent to earth as the spirit children of heavenly parents. We come here to learn and grow, and the essential circumstance for our success is human freedom of choice. We gain wisdom as we make choices throughout our lives and try to make sense of the consequences of our decisions. But all of us make at least some bad decisions that lead us to hurt other people either because in our ignorance we speak and behave in hurtful

ways or because our selfishness leads us to prioritize our own desires over the needs of others. We belittle our partners; we neglect
our neighbors; and we perpetuate economic systems that make it
nearly impossible for our sisters and brothers throughout the world
to escape poverty's dehumanizing morass.

I recognize that if God interfered with our freedom of
choice we would be less able to hurt one another through our
misguided applications of ideology and power. But under these
conditions, our will would be compromised. The forest would be
free of ogres and demons, but a little girl would never exercise her
courage to run a sylvan gauntlet in search of help for her grandfather. If God were the acting president of my church, some policies would probably be different. But I believe that those people,
mostly men, who currently run the church do so under God's in-
spiration. God guides them while still providing them with opportunities to grow through the exercise of their free will. These
same conditions exist for me and every other person who supports these men as spiritual leaders.

Because of human involvement, there are no perfect institutions, and I do not expect my church to be one. Frankly, I do not
know what a perfect religious institution would be. I do know
that the LDS Church facilitates my relationship with deity in a
manner that satisfies me and sometimes leaves me awestruck. The
LDS view of a nurturing, parental God who responds to our pe-
titions informed my instinct to pray as I ran for help down that
woodland path. LDS theology that family members can be together after death has comforted me as I have mourned the
deaths of loved ones from the ranch—my grandfather, my Aunt
Nora, my grandmother, and other beloved family members. As
behaviors such as that of my sexist branch president continue to
diminish, and women's voices are increasingly represented and
valued, as they are in my current congregation and have been in
others where I have lived, I see a future of flourishing for this
church that is my spiritual home.

Twenty-Three

MARCHING IN THE LIGHT OF GOD

Heather Grace Shortlidge

*Q*uestions catapulted through me. What had I gotten myself into? Was I anything like the other people in the crowd? What kind of tactics would the protestors of the protestors use? And where could one get some strong coffee on this early Sunday morning, April 25, 2004? I was just one of thousands of people convening in Washington, D.C., for the March for Women's Lives, one of the largest women's rights marches in more than ten years. Women and their various entourages engulfed me as I merged onto the sidewalk: toddlers nestled in strollers, elderly couples clinging to walkers, women stealing kisses with women, pregnant protruding bellies, a vibrant rainbow of races and classes, fathers and brothers and husbands and sons hanging on for dear life.

Excitement coursed through my veins. I had been anticipating the March for Women's Lives for several months, actively advertising around my seminary community, inviting friends, and especially talking it up to male colleagues and professors. I invited most of the male seminary administrators and all of my male friends to merge their faith and footsteps for the sake of women the world over. None actually accepted the invitation, but the task of naming my beliefs and asking others to march in support of them only deepened my already strong conviction that faith without taking a stand, faith without activism for the oppressed, faith without love for the other, is hardly the faith to which God calls us.

I had traveled alone via the metro from my sister's apartment in Arlington, planning on meeting friends closer to the hub of march activities. At the time she suggested that I catch a cab, but I knew that I wanted to be a part of the frenzy, not separated from the crowd by a silencing windowpane. I wanted to be fed from the passion of the crowd as well as to contribute my own nourishing passion. And what better place to people-watch than in the metro where groups excitedly chattered away, displaying their beliefs with pride. But my own bubble of fervor quickly fizzled. As I patiently waded through the zigzagging crowds, my initial excitement dissolved into a growing uneasiness. Glaring stares rocketed toward me as I jockeyed for a position inside a metro car. With no seats available, I planted myself next to a pole, contemplating the looks that completely gobbled up my enthusiasm. The fire engine red t-shirt I had carefully chosen for the event was garnering more attention than I had ever anticipated. In white lettering, the words "God bless the people of *every* nation" were positioned next to a white dove. The shirt, acquired from my days as a ministry team member at Montreat, summed up my strong feelings about the (mis)treatment of men and women around the world, America's lack of relationship with the other, and the necessity of full personhood for all people. It was one of the few t-shirts in my wardrobe that I could wear and completely own the message. Unfortunately, the eyes of protesters seized upon the word "God" and jumped to automatic assumptions about my anti-abortion, antiwomen, antimarch position. Never before had I been so conscious of the instant judgment we offer those that we do not know, conscious of and cornered by the bitter religious distaste simmering within my more progressive peers.

Each time wandering, judging eyes would lock upon the "God" so blatantly displayed for all to see, I sucked in my breath, refusing the tides of circulation until those eyes cautiously continued reading. I nervously awaited an approving smile, that small nod of acceptance. I coveted even an upturned brow or a confused gaze. Anything but rejection. Anything but a hostile stare that would bore through my being, pinning down my faith, squishing my beliefs into a jumbled chaos that churned within me. One young woman disgustingly yelled across the aisle, "God doesn't belong at this march." I was so shocked that a stranger was addressing me, accusing me, antagonizing me that it took a few seconds for her words to sink in fully. Aghast at the silence that fell upon the car and the heavy expectation of a response, I quickly racked my seminary-trained brain for an adequate answer. What to say that would be an authentic representation of me, but non-hostile? Did she even know who my God was? Who was she to judge who was and was not allowed to participate in such a march? I mumbled a quick pleading prayer to my unwelcome God and never losing contact with her piercing brown eyes said, "I had hoped that this was not an invitation-only kind of event." At that moment, the train stopped and a new hoard of people pushed their way into the car, disconnecting me from my accuser.

I longed to throw other words at her, words that sped through my mind, racing around corners and through stop signs, words and questions that greatly unsettled me. "I think my God is here whether I bring her or not. I think my God is in each and everyone of us, inside the boat we're rocking but also responsible for many of the waves that are rocking the boat. Do you worship a Divine being? Is he or she allowed? We're marching to end exclusion, not promote it! Aren't you contradicting yourself? You don't even know who I am. Is it too late to erase my faith claim, turn my t-shirt inside out, and hide my faith from the world? No one else intervened in the verbal challenge. Does everyone on this train feel the same way? Is everyone renouncing the importance of God, of faith, of the spirituality of whole lives? What was I doing here? Why did I even think this had been a good idea?"

My mother's and sister's expressed aversions of the march came back to taunt me. I envied their comfortable position, relaxing inside their carefully cloistered homes on this beautiful morning. Salvaging what little idealism I had left, I raced out of the station and swallowed as much fresh air as my lungs could take. I raced to the prearranged meeting point at New York Avenue Presbyterian Church and awaited the arrival of my friends of faith. At least my t-shirt didn't seem so outrageous with the shadow of a church steeple towering over me. At least I felt safe on the sidewalk that guided worshippers into a sanctuary where God's name was holy and revered.

I tried to stow the jarring metro ride for later reflection and to absorb the rest of the march. My senses were assaulted by slogans, loud chants, and the bustle of bodies all around me. Older white men, children of all shapes and sizes, young women, loud women, grandmothers, husbands and boyfriends, blind and hearing impaired persons, trendy people and the not-so-trendy. I wondered about each person's story and the journey that led her or him to this place. Seminarian friends, some sporting the same red t-shirt, surrounded me as we began the slow, long walk down the mall. Interestingly enough, when seen together many people smiled and complimented the message of peace to all people. But even with a supporting cast of friends and more positive vibes, it was hard to shake the earlier incident and other antifaith ones that followed. My faith and political convictions were conflicted again when I spied a pack of skinheads shoving forward signs that read, "Kill Christians." Why such senselessness? I wasn't arguing for the death of prolifers. I was advocating for options and choice, not for the murder of those who disagreed with me. Did these skinheads know any Christians? They surely did not know me or the bristle of my skin as the reality of someone wanting to kill me, because of my religion, sunk in.

At the same time that swells of exuberance cascaded through me, eddies of disappointment lingered upon the shores of my soul. In the days before the march, I had engaged in some verbal sparring with seminary colleagues who opposed the event. A few students were outraged that a faithful female would view this demonstration as prowoman. And their accusations that I had misrepresented the march in campus advertising seemed to be coming true. All along I had been describing the protest as the chance to walk in solidarity for all women all over the world. Knowing the dangers and ineffectiveness of being a single-issue activist, I consciously moved past the plethora of abortion rights material and dreamed about the other women's issues that were near and dear to my heart: women in the military, single mothers, low-wage working women, minority women, accessible and affordable health care for women, the challenges of child care, female genital mutilation, domestic violence, sexual harassment, the invisible women. It was clear to me that I was marching for more than one reason. Yet by the end of the day it was obvious that most people were marching only for that one reason: abortion rights. As the throng of marchers plodded along carrying me with them, my heart became more and more troubled. I felt like the odd-person out, the one in the middle who stuck out like a sore thumb, a person of faith who had no home, not in the church or as an activist within the protest. At one point my eyes connected with a few purple signs for the profamily, profaith, prochoice religious consortium. And I knew that somewhere in the crowd prochoice Catholics were marching because I had met a few the day before. But that hardly stopped the feelings of isolation that swelled within me.

Within the first hour of the march, it became glaringly clear that I didn't belong on either side of the barricades. For me, the march was a shouting match. There was no listening. There was no connection. There was no relationship. Dialogue was not part of the march vocabulary, and I was probably a bit naïve to think it would be. For four hours I took a stand for women's lives marching within the barricades as a woman of faith, listening to prochoice protestors scream at prolife protestors and vice versa. Through the din of voices, I could not help but think that there had to be a better way. How did we get to a point where men and women aggressively maim each other with words? Where did I belong in this shouting match? Most of the people expressing any kind of faith were stationed on the other side of the barricades, pleading with people to repent from their sins and turn to God. I was certainly advocating for God's involvement, but I surely did not belong next to men and women, mostly men, who chose to use the Bible and their particular dogma as weapons of mass destruction.

At the end of the march, my friends and I scoured the trash piles in search of cool signs to take home as souvenirs. Amidst the looming pile of "Stop the War on Women" signs, I noticed a battered pair of rouge-smeared lips with the words "Speak out against Fundamentalism." My hand reached for the small sign, and I carried it home with me. These red lips remain posted above my computer screen often producing more questions than answers. How exactly does a faithful person condemn fundamentalism? These liberating lips continue to elevate my belief in the need for dialogue between women and their various faith traditions, conversations that seek to end the vicious forces of dualism that trap all women into either/or situations. At the march, clearly one was either prochoice or prolife. The urgency, created or real, allowed for no middle ground, no wishy-washiness as my younger sister would say. In the camp that I chose to rest my head in, there was little, if any, room for religion. The other side seemed to be all about religion, leaving me with feelings of guilt for not highlighting more of my faith. Unfortunately, both the prochoice and prolife sides were debilitated and weakened by fundamentalism. Each side was guilty of a faith without love that fed the beast of fanaticism. Living with my faith and inherent interest in the equal treatment of women, in the sanctity and independence of women's bodies, and in the full personhood of all people has never been easy. Marching in Washington was a humbling reminder of just how hard it is.

Writing, solid friends, a constant quest for knowledge, self-excavation, and an awareness of the other help me in the daily struggle of navigating the discrepancies of life, the paradox of both a radical faith and a radical belief in the inherent goodness of women. Making sense of the pathologies of life is not something one accomplishes in college or with the granting of a seminary degree; it is not something that automatically occurs once one lives on her own or secures that diamond ring. Making sense of the world happens over a lifetime, and I am just getting started. Part and parcel of answering the questions is asking the questions, stirring up the sediment lodged in complacent souls, stretching people who need stretching, and taking stands on life and death issues. Part and parcel of answering the questions is carving out new spaces for both faith and feminism, living in those spaces long enough for others to join us, and dreaming up new spaces while at the same time imagining how to connect the new and old together. God is in all of those spaces while, at the same time, working through us to create such spaces. Let the fun and the love and the work begin and continue, now and forever always, amen.

In Search of Tensegrity

DISCUSSION QUESTIONS

1. In what ways do you feel that your life is balanced? In what ways would you like to achieve more balance in your life?
2. Identify areas in your life where you have to hold together competing tensions. What is your emotional reaction to this task? Do you find strength or difficulty in balancing these tensions?
3. Describe a particular situation in your life that illustrates the idea of tensegrity.
4. What does it mean to you to live in paradox?
5. What are the advantages of living in tensegrity? What are the disadvantages?
6. Who are the role models in your life who provide examples of how to hold paradoxes in a positive way?
7. Can you completely reconcile your faith and your feminism? If not, what remains in tension?
8. How can we create community among those of us who want to embrace the full complexity of life in a society that seems to desire easy solutions and right answers to every dilemma?

ACTION ACTIVITIES

1. Pick a particularly divisive issue that our nation currently debates in black and white terms. Some examples include abortion, how to reduce consumption of foreign oil, how to combat terrorism, and what to do about health care. Think about the nuances of the issue. Discuss the issue with someone else or a group of people, being careful to consider all sides and angles of the issue. Try not to polarize into two sides. Instead, try to create a solution that would respect the complexity of the situation.

2. Take time to talk to a woman of a different generation about her experiences with faith and feminism. Do your conclusions about the relationship of faith and feminism change after this conversation? Did she appear to be a woman who embraces tensegrity and paradox, or does she view things in more black and white terms? What did you learn from this other woman that was helpful for your own journey? What did she learn from you that was helpful for her journey?

Endnotes

FOREWORD

1. National Committee for Responsible Philanthropy, *Axis of Ideology: Conservative Foundations and Public Policy,* 2001 S. Street NW, Ste. 620, Washington, D.C. 20009, www.ncrp.org, 2004: 15, 63.

INTRODUCTION

1. bell hooks, *Feminism Is for Everybody: Passionate Politics* (Cambridge, MA: South End Press, 2000).

2. We recognize the influence of James Fowler's understanding of faith on our working definition. See James W. Fowler, *Stages of Faith: The Psychology of Human Development and the Quest for Meaning* (San Francisco: Harper & Row, 1980).

CHAPTER ONE—Heaney

1. Carolyn Heilbrun, *Writing a Woman's Life* (New York: Ballantine Books, 1988), 72.

2. Ibid., 58–59.

CHAPTER TWO—Melton

1. Ever since, God with a capital "G" has become impersonal for me, the deity of organized religion and empires. I retain belief in the divine by referring to "god," a softer and less hierarchical presence.

2. Kathryn Pyne Addelson, Martha Ackelsberg, and Shawn Pyne, "Anarchism and Feminism," in *Feminism and Philosophy: Essential Readings in Theory, Reinterpretation, and Application,* ed. Nancy Tuana and Rosemarie Tong (Boulder, CO: Westview Press, 1995), 330–52.

CHAPTER THREE—Gavin

1. Betty Friedan, *The Feminine Mystique* (New York: Norton, 1963).

CHAPTER SIX—Irwin

1. Gay/lesbian/bisexual/transgender/queer.

2. This summary is loosely based on the writing of Jacques Derrida, *Limited Inc.* (Evanston, IL: Northwestern University Press, 1988).
3. Michel Foucault quoted in James Miller, *The Passion of Michel Foucault* (Cambridge, MA: Harvard University Press, 1993), 19.

CHAPTER SEVEN—Roscher

1. Kathleen Norris, *Amazing Grace: A Vocabulary of Faith* (New York: Riverhead Books, 1998), 259.
2. Serene Jones, *Feminist Theory and Christian Theology: Categories of Grace* (Minneapolis: Fortress Press, 2000), 168.
3. Norris, *Amazing Grace,* 261.
4. Philippians 2:5–11.
5. Diana Lipton and Janet Martin Soskice, *Feminism and Theology* (New York: Oxford University Press, 2003), 320.

CHAPTER EIGHT—Rice

1. Carol Lakey Hess, *Caretakers of Our Common House: Women's Development in Communities of Faith* (Nashville: Abingdon Press, 1997), 129.
2. Elizabeth Cady Stanton, *The Woman's Bible* (New York: Arno Press, 1974), 11.

CHAPTER TEN—Simpson

1. Mos Def, "Umi Says," *Black on Both Sides* (Rawkus, 2002).

CHAPTER TWELVE—Brorsen

1. Sallie McFague, *Metaphorical Theology: Models of God in Religious Language* (Philadelphia: Fortress Press, 1982).
2. Rainer Maria Rilke, *Letters to a Young Poet,* trans. Stephen Mitchell (New York: Random House, 1984), 34.
3. Hildegard of Bingen, *Selected Writings,* trans. Mark Atherton (Toronto: Penguin Group, 2001), 172.

CHAPTER FOURTEEN—Copeland and Thorvilson

1. Ephesians 5:22–24.

CHAPTER SEVENTEEN—Gaffron

1. I prefer to use this more inclusive spelling of God because it offers me the opportunity to think of God with abstract instead of gendered imagery.
2. Fluxus, an association formed in the early 1960s, integrated multiple visual art forms with a performance or "happening" and relied on audience participation for the full realization of the piece. Yoko Ono's "Cut Piece" (1964) is an example of Fluxus art.

3. The Bauhaus, founded in Germany in 1919, was an art and design school based on the premise that craftsmanship is the basis of every art. Faculty such as Ludwig Mies van der Rohe, Wassily Kandinsky, and Paul Klee were innovators in modern art. See Klaus Richter, *Art from Impressionism to the Internet* (Munich: Prestel Sightlines, 2001), for further information.

4. These quotations are from a lecture given by Dr. Wilson Yates at United Theological Seminary in the course "Theological Interpretations of the Arts" on November 2, 2004.

5. Robin M. Jensen, *The Substance of Things Seen: Art, Faith and the Christian Community* (Grand Rapids, MI: William B. Eerdmans, 2004).

6. Ibid., 12.

7. Ibid.

8. Ibid., 78.

9. Ibid., 75–100.

10. Deborah Haynes, *Art Lessons: Meditations on the Creative Life* (Boulder, CO: Westview Press, 2003).

11. Ibid., 176.

CHAPTER NINETEEN—Brock

1. John 13:34.

2. From *The Book of Common Prayer* (New York: Church Publishing, 1979), 324. See also Matthew 22:37–40, Mark 12:29–31, Luke 10:27–28, Leviticus 19:18, and Deuteronomy 6:4–5.

3. Genesis 1:27–28.

4. John 15:12.

CHAPTER TWENTY—Kim-Cragg

1. Since the suicide of the young labor worker Jeon Tai-Il in 1970, many young Koreans have given up their lives as a way of protest. My colleague, Park Hyun-Min, however, was the first and last university student from the Student Christian Movement to take his life away for peace and democracy.

2. South Korea was becoming wealthier, while the labor conditions of workers were becoming worse than in the 1980s under the military regime, which abused political power at the expense of human rights and democracy. The national division between South and North was manipulated by both governments, which only contributed to heavy militarization, far from bringing peace on earth in Korea.

3. A university student, Lee Han-Yol, was killed by a direct hit from a tear gas canister in 1987, which brought millions of people out to the protest and finally led to the Korean civil movement called June 10 of 1987.

4. C. Austin Miles, "I Come to the Garden Alone," 1913.

5. I intentionally use "becoming" in order to emphasize the process of my identity as a feminist Christian continually forming and reforming. I was inspired by the view of "becoming" suggested by the International Steering Group of the World Council of Churches on the Asian Women's Theological Consultation in Seoul, Korea, October 24–28, 2000. See *In God's Image* 23:1 (March 2004), 61–64.

6. Leonila V. Bermisa writes about a feminist approach to justice as the establishment of just relationships between women and men and between humans and the ecological community. See Leonila V. Bermisa, "Word, Sacrament, and Liturgy: Philippine Experience," *In God's Image* 23:1 (March 2004), 50–56.

CHAPTER TWENTY-ONE—Andrew

1. Mary Oliver, "Wild Geese," *Dream Work* (New York: Atlantic Monthly Press, 1986), 14.

2. Annie Dillard, *Holy the Firm* (New York: Harper & Row, 1977), 11.

3. Matthew Fox, *Original Blessing: A Primer in Creation Spirituality Presented in Four Paths, Twenty-Six Themes, and Two Questions* (Santa Fe, NM: Bear & Co., 1983).

4. St. John of the Cross, *Dark Night of the Soul,* trans. Mirabai Starr (New York: Riverhead Books, 2002), 68.

5. Ibid., 67.

6. Ibid., 68.

7. Ibid., 96.

8. Ibid.

9. Ibid., 24.

10. Carter Heyward, *Touching Our Strength: The Erotic as Power and the Love of God* (San Francisco: Harper San Francisco, 1989).

11. St. John, *Dark Night,* 24.

12. Ibid., 56.

13. J. M. Cohen, *The Life of Saint Teresa of Avila by Herself* (New York: Penguin Books, 1957).

14. St. John, *Dark Night,* 182.

15. Ibid., 23.

CHAPTER TWENTY-TWO—Holbrook

1. Mormonism teaches of a Mother in heaven as well, but we are instructed to pray to our Father. The most common belief is that Father in heaven thinks so highly of Mother that he does not want us to know too much about her, for fear we would profane her (as so many do him).

2. King James Version.

3. The assertion that women do not hold leadership positions in the church is not strictly true. Women do not have positions in which they direct the actions of men, but the leaders of auxiliary organizations for women, adolescent females, and children are always women.

4. The actions of this particular branch president would likely have been frowned upon by church leadership. Not only are church members instructed to reprimand in private, but male leaders are expected to include women in their meetings: "The sisters who serve as leaders need to be invited to participate and to be listened to and included in our state and ward council meetings" (James E. Faust, "Keeping Covenants and Honoring the Priesthood," *Ensign* November 1993, 36). Further, in 1979 President Spencer W. Kimball told the men in the church, "Our sisters do not wish to be indulged or to be treated condescendingly; they desire to be respected and revered as our sisters and our equals. I mention all these things, my brethren, not because the doctrines or the teachings of the Church regarding women are in any doubt, but because in some situations our behavior is of doubtful quality." Spencer W. Kimball, "Our Sisters in the Church," *Ensign* (November 1979), 48. Nonetheless, if women held higher positions of leadership, and if I had not been the only woman in that room, my branch president would not have been able to justify his behavior as he did.

5. Juliet Schor, *Overworked American: The Unexpected Decline of Leisure* (New York: Basic Books, 1991).

Author Biographies

SADIE ACKERMAN has degrees in religious studies and creative writing from the University of Arizona. She recently relocated to North Carolina, where her husband accepted a professorship in the music department of the University of North Carolina, Wilmington. She writes in the summers when he is around to finger-paint and make juice popsicles for their two sons, Ellis (age six) and Thayer (age three).

ELIZABETH J. ANDREW is the author of *Swinging on the Garden Gate: A Spiritual Memoir* (Boston: Skinner House Books, 2000), *Writing the Sacred Journey: The Art and Practice of Spiritual Memoir* (Boston: Skinner House Books, 2005), and *On the Threshold: Home, Hardwood, and Holiness* (Cambridge, MA: Westview Press, 2005). She teaches creative writing at the Loft Literary Center, United Theological Seminary, and various religious communities in the Twin Cities, Minnesota.

CLAIRE BISCHOFF recently completed an M.A. in educational leadership at Luther Seminary and ended her three-year tenure as coordinator of religious formation for children and youth at a Catholic parish in St. Paul, the city she considers home. She is currently living in Atlanta, Georgia, with her husband while pursuing a Ph.D. in religious education and practical theology at Emory University, and she hopes one day to land her dream job as a professor of religion.

MARY LOUISE BOZZA graduated from Boston College in 2003 with a degree in theology and Hispanic studies and completed a senior thesis project on Dorothy Day. After graduation, she served for two years as a member of a volunteer program in Chicago, teaching world religions and helping in the urban studies, community service, and pastoral ministry programs at a Jesuit high school. She is originally from Connecticut.

THE REV. LAURIE BROCK is an Episcopal priest currently serving a parish in Alabama. She is a graduate of the General Theological Seminary in New York City. Prior to her ordination, she was an attorney with legal services. When not celebrating mass, she works with youth and social justice ministries.

CAROL BRORSEN is editor of *Uprising* magazine, www.uprisingmag.com, which seeks to cultivate hope and community among progressive, spiritual young adults. Carol, thirty-four, is a recent graduate of Episcopal Divinity School, Cambridge, Massachusetts, where she received a master of divinity degree with a focus on feminist and queer theologies.

ADAM J. COPELAND recently graduated from St. Olaf College with a degree in English and religion. While a student, Adam traveled on the Global Semester, served on the College Honor Council, and sang in the St. Olaf Choir. Adam also served as comoderator of the National Presbyterian Youth Council from 2000 to 2003. He plans to become a Presbyterian pastor.

THE REV. MARYANN MCKIBBEN DANA is a Presbyterian minister, writer, and knitter of splendidly imperfect projects. She authors a weblog called "reverendmother," where she writes about her adventures in pastoring and parenting. She lives in the Virginia suburbs of Washington, D.C., with her husband, Robert, and daughter, Caroline, known affectionately and reverently as "she who is."

RACHEL GAFFRON is a writer and visual artist living in Minneapolis, Minnesota. In 2004, she was awarded a residency at Norcroft: A Writing Retreat for Women and was selected to participate in the Loft Literary Center's Mentor Series for emerging writers. She is also pursuing an M.A. in theology and the arts at United Theological Seminary of the Twin Cities. Her passions include the study and expression of the creative synthesis between art, spirituality, and social justice.

MEGAN BURON GAVIN has a B.A. in international affairs and linguistics from the University Professors Program at Boston University, as well as an M.A. in Hispanic language and literature. She has studied and worked in Europe, Central America, and West Africa and is a polyglot, an optimist, and a good cook.

KATIE HAEGELE lives in Philadelphia, where she works as an essayist and freelance journalist. Her work has appeared recently in *The Philadelphia Inquirer, The Utne Reader,* and the fiction anthology *Women Behaving Badly* (Wake Forest, NC: Paper Journey Press, 2004).

APRIL HEANEY earned an M.A. in creative writing from the University of Wyoming in 2000 and currently teaches in the English department. Her work has appeared in *American Nature Writing 2003, Mudrock: Stories and Tales, FMAM Magazine,* and the *Owen Wister Review.*

KATHLEEN HOLBROOK has an M.A. in theological studies from Harvard Divinity School and is currently pursuing a Ph.D. in religion and litera- ture with a focus on women's spirituality and domesticity from Boston University. She is an editor for the Church of Jesus Christ of Latter-Day Saints' feminist journal *Exponent II* and lives in Boston with her husband and two young daughters.

THE REV. SARA IRWIN is the assistant rector at Emmanuel Church, an Episcopal parish in Boston, Massachusetts. A graduate of New College of Florida and General Theological Seminary (New York, NY), she is inter- ested in postmodernism and liberation theology and in urban and young adult ministry.

THE REV. HYERAN KIM-CRAGG was born in Korea and is now living in Canada as a wife of a minister and a mother of Noah and Hannah. She is an ordained minister and currently writing a Th.D. dissertation in religious education from a postcolonial perspective in the Toronto School of Theology.

MONICA ANN MAESTRAS is a thirty-year-old woman living in Albuquerque, New Mexico, with her husband, Brian, where they are planning to adopt their first child. She considers herself to be a spiritual person who identifies Catholicism as her primary source of spirituality, among other sources. Monica works part-time as a vocational coordina- tor for homeless women, and she is also a writer and a student. She has a B.A. in psychology and is working on an M.A. in secondary teaching. Monica particularly enjoys spending time with her family and friends, as well as pursuing her interests in music, poetry, literature, and art.

ANN CREWS MELTON hails from Longview, Texas, and is currently ab- sorbing the bluegrass, bourbon, and Benedictine canapés of Louisville, Kentucky. She enjoys cutting up magazines, photocopying, and drawing maps of the universe for her zine, *Red Milk.*

CHRISTIANA Z. PEPPARD is a water-loving biologist-turned-ethicist who is currently a Ph.D. student in religious ethics at Yale University and an editor at Yale University's Interdisciplinary Bioethics Project. She plans to pursue teaching at the college level.

KELSEY RICE currently works with a Christian feminist organization in Louisville, Kentucky, the National Network of Presbyterian College Women, which empowers women as leaders in the church and society. Before landing a job she loves, Kelsey graduated with a B.A. in history and English literature from Whitworth College in Spokane, Washington.

ELLIE ROSCHER received her B.A. in religion from Gustavus Adolphus College in St. Peter, Minnesota. After a year of volunteering in the Urban Servant Corps, she proceeded to Luther Seminary in St. Paul, Minnesota, where she earned her M.A. in theology, specializing in urban ministry. She currently is completing another year of volunteer work, this time in an after-school program in Rocha, Uruguay, through the Evangelical Lutheran Church in America's (ELCA) Division of Global Ministry.

HEATHER SCHEIWE grew up in Fort Collins, Colorado. Most recently, she graduated from St. Olaf College with an independent major in narrative understanding of religious identity and traditional degrees in women's studies and religion. She is the founder and editor of *Alive Magazine,* an alternative Christian publication by and for young women.

A delver into complexities. A justice-oriented czarina. A feminist committed to not having her faith diluted. **HEATHER GRACE SHORTLIDGE** currently serves as a chaplain resident at the Children's Medical Center of Dallas. She loves newspapers, books of all kinds, ballet, baking, trying new restaurants, and asking big questions. Heather received her undergraduate degree from the Jepson School of Leadership Studies at the University of Richmond and her Masters of Divinity from Union Theological Seminary and Presbyterian School of Christian Education. Heather dedicates her voice to Dr. Katie Geneva Cannon, a gifted teacher in the delicate balance of faith and activism. Dr. Cannon listened and heard her story into speech. For that she is most thankful.

MONIQUE SIMPSON'S favorite question is "Why?" Her quest for a better understanding of society and women's roles in it has led her to study sociology at the University of California Los Angeles (UCLA) and gender studies at the University of Southern California (USC). She is currently working on her first nonfiction book, *Oprah's Sorority: A New Kind of Sisterhood,* as part of her graduate thesis in the Master of Professional Writing Program at USC. Simpson resides in Los Angeles but plans to live in Japan soon.

MEGAN J. THORVILSON grew up in rural North Dakota. She graduated from St. Olaf College in Northfield, Minnesota, with a degree in biology in 2003. She currently studies at Luther Seminary in St. Paul, Minnesota, pursuing a Master of Divinity degree.